Ronald Rea...

DECISIONS OF GREATNESS

Ronald Reagan

DECISIONS OF GREATNESS

Martin Anderson & Annelise Anderson

HOOVER INSTITUTION PRESS

Stanford University | *Stanford, California*

The Hoover Institution on War, Revolution and Peace, founded at
Stanford University in 1919 by Herbert Hoover, who went on to become
the thirty-first president of the United States, is an interdisciplinary
research center for advanced study on domestic and international affairs.
The views expressed in its publications are entirely those of the authors
and do not necessarily reflect the views of the staff, officers, or Board of
Overseers of the Hoover Institution.

www.hoover.org

Hoover Institution Press Publication No. 657

Hoover Institution at Leland Stanford Junior University, Stanford,
California 94305-6010

First printing 2015
21   9 8 7 6 5 4 3

Manufactured in the United States of America

The paper used in this publication meets the minimum Requirements of the
American National Standard for Information Sciences—Permanence of Paper for
Printed Library Materials, ANSI/NISO Z39.48-1992. ♾

Cataloging-in-Publication Data is available from the Library of Congress.
ISBN 978-0-8179-1834-7 (cloth : alk. paper)
ISBN 978-0-8179-1835-4 (pbk. : alk. paper)
ISBN 978-0-8179-1836-1 (e-book)
ISBN 978-0-8179-1837-8 (mobi)
ISBN 978-0-8179-1838-5 (PDF)

For Nancy Reagan and George Shultz

Contents

[Illustrations follow pages 40 and 88.]

Foreword

In *Ronald Reagan: Decisions of Greatness*, Martin and Annelise Anderson bring a lifetime of factual inquiry and critical thinking to bear arguably on the pivotal achievement of Reagan's presidency—ending the Cold War. While the Soviet Union did not cease to exist as a rival superpower until 1991, signaling the formal end of the Cold War, the Andersons demonstrate how decisions Reagan made as far back as the first year of his presidency set the stage for drastic nuclear arms reduction in the late 1980s and beyond. Indeed, it was Reagan's firm conviction that a nuclear war could not be won and must never be fought that permeated his efforts to negotiate peace through strength.

As a treatise focused specifically on Reagan's vision and strategy for arms reduction, *Ronald Reagan: Decisions of Greatness* helps to further define and clarify the legacy of Ronald Reagan. We are indebted to Martin and Annelise for continuing to mine the writings of Reagan, presenting to the public at large a clearer, more accurate portrayal of this great man. Through such works as *Reagan, In His Own Hand* (2001), with Kiron K. Skinner, and *Reagan: A Life in Letters* (2004), with Skinner, each with a foreword by George P. Shultz, the Andersons have clearly revealed Reagan as the intellectual driver of his administration's initiatives and strategies. One could argue their writings and publication of Reagan's own words played no small part in the public's increasing admiration for President Reagan.

I take great pleasure in participating in this effort of publishing and releasing on behalf of the Hoover Institution. Both Martin and Annelise served in the Reagan Administration and have been affiliated with Hoover as fellows going back as early as 1971. Both have been invaluable colleagues who have contributed to the intellectual rigor and profile of the Hoover Institution through their longtime dedicated service. Martin and Annelise are dear friends, partners in policy research, and patriots in the pursuit of freedom worldwide. I trust you will find much to appreciate in this book.

JOHN RAISIAN
Tad and Dianne Taube Director
Hoover Institution, Stanford University

Preface

This book includes a great deal that is new in the process of telling the story of Ronald Reagan's primary accomplishment: persuading the Soviets to reduce their nuclear arsenals and end the Cold War. It challenges, with documents and evidence, two views of Reagan that have become more common: that he would not have retaliated against a Soviet nuclear attack; and that he changed his views and his strategy toward the Soviet Union halfway through his presidency.

Reagan learned in his initial year as president that if the Soviets attacked the United States, 150 million Americans would be killed—and so, probably, would he, in the first six to eight minutes of the attack. Some of his colleagues have speculated that his horror of war—and especially nuclear war—was so great that he would not have retaliated against such an attack. But this book demonstrates, in interviews, documents, and diplomatic exchanges, that Reagan would most certainly have retaliated with the full force at his command. "It had to be," he told Martin Anderson, one of the co-authors of this volume, not once but twice, in the summer after leaving the presidency.

While the country was concentrating on reviving the US economy—a critical component of a convincing military stand—Reagan was also taking the steps to strengthen US military morale, manpower, training, and equipment to make it possible to convince the Soviets that they could not win a nuclear war and that such a war would be devastating to both sides. On April 17, 1982, Reagan made his first definitive statement that "nuclear war cannot be won and must never be fought."

The Soviets built nuclear weapons—first five hundred a year, then one thousand, then two thousand—right through the first year of Mikhail Gorbachev's rule. The Carter presidency had left the Soviets with 25 percent more nuclear weapons than the United States held, and the disparity expanded under Reagan's tenure through 1985. But by the end of 1981, Reagan got the MX (Peacekeeper) missile, the improved Trident D-5 missiles for submarines, and the B-1 and Stealth bombers approved and on the drawing boards, although the basing of the MX remained a matter of contention. In March 1983, he introduced the Strategic Defense Initiative, a program of then-unknown outcome but one the Soviets had no way to counter. In late 1983, following persistent efforts to work with America's allies, the Pershing II and cruise missiles were introduced into Western Europe. "They are a gun to our temple," Gorbachev would tell his advisors.

Reagan's ultimate goal—the dream, as he called it—was the complete elimination of nuclear weapons and much greater reliance on defense against missiles rather than retaliation. In the meantime, he focused immediate efforts on ensuring the effectiveness of the US nuclear deterrent. The MX itself was partly designed to make the Soviet leaders realize—which they hadn't until then—that they, too, would meet their demise in a nuclear war, so powerful and precise was that weapon. Thus they also adopted—at Geneva and in individual statements—the view that a nuclear war could not be won and must never be fought. They came to that realization even as Reagan, through strategic defense, sought an alternative to make nuclear missiles obsolete and thus eliminate the possibility of an all-out nuclear war.

It is this accomplishment, certainly underpinned by the economic might of the United States, that the authors believe led to the increasing respect for Reagan. That became especially true as the public became more aware of how much of the strategy and negotiating was planned and carried out by Reagan himself, and it led to his popular standing as "the greatest US president."

Chapter 1 brings together the record on Americans' view of Reagan as a great president. We explore why it took so long for the public to give him credit for his accomplishments.

Chapter 2 is a summary of Reagan's unique accomplishment: persuading the Soviets to reverse the systematic, decades-long buildup of their nuclear arsenal.

Chapter 3 recounts how Reagan found out, in a classified National Security Council meeting on December 3, 1981, that if the Soviets attacked the United States, 150 million residents—65 percent of the population—would be killed. Although he never mentioned this in public, he did note it in his personal diary.

This chapter continues with selections from Martin Anderson's interview with Reagan on July 25, 1989, in which Reagan twice tells Anderson that if the Soviets attacked, the United States would retaliate. Reagan makes clear in the interview that the Soviets were well aware that he would take this action, even though, according to projections, he himself would quickly be killed.

Chapter 4 presents a year-by-year graph of US and Soviet nuclear warheads since 1945. The chapter recounts the development of US and Soviet nuclear arsenals from the Truman years through the Carter years, showing in each period what Reagan was doing, specifically how he was involved in one way or another in US foreign affairs and the nuclear age. Concluding with a section on Reagan, the chapter tracks the steady buildup of Soviet nuclear warheads until the reversal and the arsenal's subsequent decline during the Reagan presidency.

Chapter 5 reviews the decisions Reagan made during his presidency that made his success possible. The analysis emphasizes the fact that by the end of 1981, his policies and strategy were in place, in contrast to the view of some writers that Reagan changed course in his second term.

Chapters 6 and 7 review Reagan's critical negotiations with Soviet leader Gorbachev.

Chapter 8 recounts Reagan's conclusion about the end of the Cold War: "Freedom won, as we always knew it would."

Chapter 9 quotes Gorbachev on Reagan as a great man and a great president—twenty years after Reagan left office.

Chapter 10 reviews the status of nuclear arsenals under post-Reagan presidents.

Chapter 11 summarizes Reagan's contribution to reducing nuclear arsenals, encouraging missile defense, and envisioning a way to eliminate nuclear weapons.

The black-and-white photo section illustrates primarily events in Reagan's presidency. Color photographs of sixteen original one-sheet movie posters from the authors' collection are included in the color photo section. Reagan made fifty-three feature films during his acting career; Nancy Reagan (as Nancy Davis) made twelve.

Appendix A includes the full text of the Anderson-Reagan interview in 1989, conducted a few months after Reagan left the presidency.

Appendix B, by nuclear weapons expert Lowell Wood, describes the strategic nuclear situation Reagan faced as he took the job of president on January 20, 1981.

Our goal in this book is to explain not only why Americans consider Reagan one of our greatest presidents but also to explain how he achieved his greatest accomplishment. In so doing, we look primarily, as we always have in our work, to the man's own words.

Acknowledgments

Our primary debt in writing this book goes to Ronald Reagan, who during his long career took up his pen to write his own speeches, two autobiographies, 686 radio commentaries, and some ten thousand letters. He also spoke extemporaneously to the press, to students, and to other groups; and he expressed his own views freely in National Security Council meetings that were, at the time, classified.

Kirstin Julian was our archivist and research assistant for several years. Her skills and hard work were a great help in putting this book together. She is a trained archivist who kept track of the many collections of papers we have acquired or created over the years. She also put together the photos of posters and stills included in the photo sections of this book, and prepared the chart on nuclear arsenals of the United States and the Soviet Union. She tracked down a great deal of data—not only the most recent available data on the nuclear arsenals but also polling data and presidential statements. She also helped assemble the posters and other materials from the authors' collection that were displayed at the Bohemian Club in 2011.

Heather Campbell compiled the original information on what Ronald Reagan was doing during the 1950s and 1960s, searching online newspaper archives and other sources to create a calendar of his activities. Nick Siekierski also worked on this project.

Lowell Wood has been a long-time friend of ours. We have had many long, enjoyable, and informative discussions about nuclear weapons, strategy, and missile defense over the years. For this book, he wrote the appendix on the strategic situation Reagan confronted when he took office, an important reminder that whatever the economic difficulties they were having, the Soviets posed a real threat. He read several of our own chapters, which helped enormously. Remaining errors are, of course, ours.

We also thank Michael Boskin, John Taylor, and Darrell Trent for their enthusiasm and suggestions on various parts of the manuscript.

As always, we benefited greatly from the support of the director of the Hoover Institution, John Raisian, on this project as on many others over the years.

CHAPTER ONE

Ronald Reagan:
The View of Americans

On February 18, 2011, the headline on the Gallup Poll's news release read: *Americans Say Reagan Is the Greatest US President.* Ronald Reagan came in ahead of even Abraham Lincoln and George Washington.

Gallup, the most highly respected polling organization in the country, has often polled US residents about whom they consider the greatest president in the nation's history. Gallup has asked this "Who was the greatest president" question eight times since 1999. Reagan finished first not only in 2011, the most recent poll, but also in 2001 and 2005.[1]

Lincoln came in first in 1999, in two polls in 2003, and in 2007. Kennedy made it into first place in 2000 and tied with Lincoln in November 2003. Besides those listed in Table 1, a few other presidents get occasional mentions—but none by more than 5 percent of respondents.

Gallup's 2011 poll, the most recent because Gallup did not ask this question in the succeeding two years, was conducted February 2–5 and randomly sampled 1,015 adults, 18 years and older, living in the continental United States, a far broader selection—and one much more similar to eligible voters—than the narrow group of academic historians and political scientists who are often asked to rank US presidents. Those are the people who will be casting their ballots and deciding who will become president in the future.

As we might expect, political party preferences show up in their "greatest president" choices. Republicans, Independents, and Democrats make different judgments. What's remarkable—as Table 2 shows—is that many Independents as well as Republicans name Reagan the greatest US president. In 2011, he was the choice

TABLE 1   "Greatest President" (Percent of Respondents)

	2011	2005	2001
Ronald Reagan	19	20	18
Abraham Lincoln	14	14	14
Bill Clinton	13	15	9
John Kennedy	11	12	16
George Washington	10	5	5
Franklin Roosevelt	8	12	6

Sources: Gallup Inc., 2001, 2005, 2011.

TABLE 2   "Greatest President," by Respondents' Political Party—2011 (by Percent)

Republicans		Independents		Democrats	
Reagan	38	Lincoln	19	Clinton	22
Washington	14	Reagan	16	Kennedy	18
Lincoln	13	Clinton	11	Obama	11
Kennedy	7	Washington	10	F. Roosevelt	10
G.W. Bush	5	F. Roosevelt	9	Lincoln	10

Source: Gallup Inc., 2011.

of 38 percent of Republicans and second only to Lincoln among Independents.[2]

In an article about the 2011 poll results, Gallup's Frank Newport pointed out that the greatest president question—always asked the same way—is open ended: respondents have to name a president rather than select from a list.[3] They are more likely to choose recent presidents who've been in the news rather than those lost in the history books.

In 2009, however, Gallup gave respondents an opportunity to select the greatest US president from a list. Reagan was selected by 24 percent, slightly edging out Kennedy and Lincoln, who each garnered 22 percent of the "votes" and came in well ahead of Franklin Roosevelt (18 percent) and even George Washington (9 percent).[4]

Gallup periodically asks another question about presidents: how people think a president will "go down in history." The choices are Outstanding, Above Average, Average, Below Average, or Poor. This was the question Gallup asked in a survey on February 2–5, 2012 (Table 3). The presidents on the list have been those who held office from Richard Nixon through Barack Obama. The question does not require a strict ranking; a respondent can predict that more than one president, or even several of them, will go down in history as outstanding. And the question focuses on "history" rather than the personal views of the responder. The result of the poll: more people thought that, in this respect, Reagan would be ranked as Outstanding or Above Average than any of his counterparts.[5]

By large margins, Reagan and Clinton lead the list. When the results are broken down by political party, Reagan is predicted to go down in history as Outstanding or Above Average by not only 90 percent of Republicans but also 70 percent of Independents and *almost half of Democrats*, illustrating that political party isn't the only criterion people consider. His appeal is broader than Clinton's. Eighty percent of Democrats think that history will judge Clinton as Outstanding or Above Average, as 61 percent of Independents have done (but only 36 percent of Republicans).[6]

TABLE 3   How the Presidents Will Go Down in History—2012 (by Percent)

	Outstanding/Above Average
Ronald Reagan	69
Bill Clinton	60
Barack Obama	38
George H.W. Bush	35
Jimmy Carter	25
George W. Bush	25
Gerald Ford	21
Richard Nixon	14

Source: Gallup Inc., 2012.

Gallup has asked this question on occasion for decades, and Reagan's ranking has increased steadily since the early 1990s. In 1993, fewer than 40 percent of respondents thought Reagan would go down in history as an Outstanding or Above Average president.[7] By the middle of the first decade of the 21st century, over 60 percent thought so,[8] and by 2012, almost 70 percent—more than any of the presidents who came after him.[9]

Another question Gallup includes on surveys involves retrospective approval ratings: whether, in retrospect, people approve or disapprove of the way previous presidents handled the job. Reagan's ratings in this category have also increased since the 1990s, from 50 percent approval to almost 75 percent, higher than any president from John Fitzgerald Kennedy onward except Kennedy himself.[10]

Gallup is not the only pollster who finds the public rating Reagan highly. Twenty-eight percent of respondents in a 2006 Quinnipiac University poll[11] said they considered him the "best president" we've had since World War II, better than Clinton (25 percent) or JFK (18 percent).[12]

In a December 2011 "60 Minutes"/*Vanity Fair* poll, respondents were asked to pick the previous president they'd most like to have running the country today. Reagan came in first overall as well as first among Republicans and Independents; Democrats chose Franklin Delano Roosevelt first and Reagan second.[13]

All polls are of course, snapshots, but a series of snapshots makes a motion picture. What we see in the Gallup polls over the years is an increasing regard for Ronald Reagan and his performance as president. Respondents across the political spectrum consider him a great president. An increasing number judge that he will go down in history as outstanding, and an increasing number approve, in retrospect, of his performance in office.

Why Recognition Took So Long

It was not until 2001 that Reagan was chosen by more people than any other president as the greatest US president. He was also their choice in 2005, 2009, and, most recently, in 2011. Yet he left office in the opening days of 1989.

For more than a decade after his two presidential terms, Reagan's reputation was primarily that of a "great communicator." From the press to the public, people wondered whether he was reading someone else's lines. Who was pulling his strings? Reagan gave a few substantial speeches—often not very different from his farewell address—and did not crow about his accomplishments in office. Like other former presidents, he commented little on current affairs, not wishing to upstage his successor. And in 1994, six years after he left office, he retired from public life.

Reagan's presidential memoir, *An American Life*,[14] came out in 1990. He told us a great deal, and the book is a basic source on his presidency. Nevertheless, reviewers criticized it for an absence of personal revelations.

The first full biography of Reagan that covered his presidency was Lou Cannon's book, *President Reagan: The Role of a Lifetime*, published in 1992. Cannon concluded then that "Reagan rarely sought to focus on higher goals. He . . . took his role too lightly. In the end, it proved too big for his talents."[15] But these words do not appear in the revised 2000 edition. Cannon had changed his mind.

Meanwhile, President Reagan's authorized biographer, Edmund Morris, was hard at work on what was expected to become one of the definitive works on the Reagan presidency. But the book, *Dutch*, was not published until 1999. Other historians had backed off, given that Morris had the inside track, making the 1990s the lost decade of Reagan scholarship. Morris introduced fictional characters and stories into the account; it was impossible to tell what was history and what was imagined.

People were still wondering who pulled Reagan's strings. Lee Edwards, journalist, public relations specialist, author of an early biography (*Reagan: A Political Biography*), and currently a fellow at the Heritage Foundation, didn't wonder. "Reagan is an open book," Edwards said, "and he's been reading it to us for years."[16] Indeed he was; virtually everything Reagan wanted to accomplish—his strategy, his vision, his ultimate goals—all are there in his writings and extemporaneous statements.

Part of the problem was that many of us weren't paying enough attention. Another part was that Reagan didn't remind people that he had, in fact, written—in his own hand—a great deal about many of the policy issues of the day. And the view persisted that whatever he was saying, he might be reading other people's lines. As it turned out, his speechwriters were carefully re-crafting Reagan's own words.

Reagan's Writings

It was not until after the turn of the century that Reagan's own extensive writings—radio commentaries, speeches, letters—began to be discovered and published. They were extensive, and they changed our view of him.

From 1975 to 1979, the years between his governorship and his presidency, Reagan had a syndicated radio-commentary program. The commentaries were about three minutes each, aired five days a week. Reagan's handwritten drafts of 686 of them were discovered in his personal collection, which is held in the Ronald Reagan Presidential Library. He wrote, by hand on yellow pads, about domestic, economic, foreign policy, and defense issues. A collection of the commentaries was published in *Reagan, In His Own Hand*[17] on February 6, 2001. Previewed by William Safire in *The New York Times Magazine*, the book quickly became a bestseller.[18]

That Reagan could write, and had written, about so many issues on the minds of Americans was news. "How come I and my colleagues never discovered these Reagan depths?"[19] Godfrey Sperling wrote in his *Christian Science Monitor* review. A second book, *Reagan's Path to Victory*,[20] included all the hand-written essays not included in the first volume.

Reagan: A Life in Letters,[21] published in September 2003 and featured on the cover of *Time*,[22] again made news: Reagan was a letter writer, writing not only to family and friends but also to Soviet leaders, US politicians like Richard Nixon, members of the press, and citizens who disagreed (or agreed) with his policies but didn't know him personally. The sheer quantity and diversity of the letters was stunning. And few had been seen before except by recipients and a few friends. The book included 1,100 letters, a selection from six thousand available at the time. The total grew: as we write now, we've found close to ten thousand letters Reagan wrote by hand or dictated on tape.

And then there was the personal diary. Almost every night during his presidency, Reagan wrote about the day's events in his diary. An excerpted, one-volume book edited by Douglas Brinkley, *The Reagan Diaries*, was not published until 2007.[23] The unabridged version, transcribing the five leather-bound books in which Reagan wrote throughout his presidency, appeared in 2009 in two long volumes.[24]

During his presidency, Reagan held more than 40 formal news conferences, broadcast live on television and radio and covered in detail in news media. But only 15 percent of his remarks to and exchanges with the press occurred in these formal settings. All the rest were less formal and structured, occurring two or three times a week with a few interviewers or a group of, say, radio broadcasters or other groups of media who weren't official White House correspondents. These interactions with the press are part of the *Public Papers of the President*,[25] but the reporting on what he said was often selective and incomplete, and reached fewer people than the formal events. They are a valuable source of his extemporaneous remarks.

There was more to come. What did Reagan tell the members of his National Security Council (NSC) or the even-more-selective National Security Planning Group in meetings where everything was classified—secret, top-secret, or even higher? Here was the president wrestling with the options and making the decisions, setting out the strategy, expressing the goals and objectives that he intended the members of the NSC and its staff to develop into detailed policies and plans of action. What each person—including the president—said in these meetings was usually carefully recorded by a scribe and became the official minutes.

Not until Martin Anderson, armed with security clearances from the Department of Defense, received permission from both the Reagans and the Bush White House to read the NSC minutes and other classified documents—memoranda of conversations, transcripts of telephone conversations with foreign leaders, and correspondence with heads of state—could all these documents, unavailable for so long, be requested for clearance and made available to those seeking to understand what Reagan was doing and how. The NSC minutes cover a wide range of issues, the most important being those on which the authors of this work focused in their 2009 book, *Reagan's Secret War: The Untold Story of His Fight to Save the World from Nuclear Disaster.*[26]

Ronald Reagan was a writer, and we cannot really know him without delving into what he himself wrote over the years. His written work encompassed serious school essays and stories, a sports column in the *Des Moines Ledger*, and feature articles for *The Des Moines Register* on becoming a Hollywood actor. He wrote his own speeches and an autobiography published in 1965, in addition to the radio commentaries, letters, and diary plus his extensive remarks and statements in NSC meetings. Many of these writings did not become available until a dozen or more years after he left the presidency, and thus were not available to his earlier biographers.

If the 1990s was the lost decade of Reagan scholarship, the first decade of the twenty-first century was the high water mark of that scholarship, the period when we came to know him through his own writings. It was only then that people began to realize that his thinking and decision making drove the events of his presidency and that he is, therefore, a great president.

CHAPTER TWO

Reagan's Unique Accomplishment

Of all Ronald Reagan's accomplishments, the most important—and unique—was persuading the Soviets to reverse their nuclear buildup and end the Cold War. He finally convinced Mikhail Gorbachev, leader of the Soviet Union, that an arms race was a contest the Soviets could not win and that a nuclear attack would be a disaster for the Soviet Union as well as the United States and Europe. The chart in Chapter 4 illustrates the systematic buildup of the Soviet nuclear arsenal in comparison to the US arsenal and the dramatic decline Reagan persuaded Soviet leaders to undertake.

Reagan accomplished many things during his presidency. He greatly improved the economy, implementing an economic policy challenged by his opponents and even those in his own administration. The success of his economic policies made it possible for him to carry out his strategy in dealing with the Soviet Union.

Well before he took office, Reagan was deeply concerned about the capability of the United States to deter a Soviet attack. He was convinced that nuclear war meant mutually assured destruction, but he did not think the Soviets were convinced that nuclear war meant destruction for *them*.

While the country was concentrating on reviving the US economy, Reagan was also taking the steps to strengthen US military morale, manpower, training, and equipment—all prerequisites to convincing the Soviets that they could not win a nuclear war. In April 1982, Reagan made his first definitive statement that "A nuclear war cannot be won and must never be fought."

From the time the Soviets acquired, in 1949, the capability to build nuclear weapons, they built steadily. Whether the United States was or was not adding to its own arsenals, the Soviets continued to build—at first five hundred a year, then one thousand, then two thousand a year—right through the first year of Gorbachev's leadership of the Soviet Union.

The total count of Soviet nuclear warheads exceeded that of the United States for the first time in 1978, during the Carter administration. When Reagan took office in 1981, the Soviets had 25 percent more nuclear warheads than did the United States: 30,665 to 24,104. The Soviet total reached an astounding 38,582 at its peak in 1985, the year Mikhail Gorbachev became general secretary of the Communist Party and therefore leader of the Soviet Union.

By contrast, Reagan did not increase the US stockpile; he actually decreased it by almost one thousand warheads. He did, however, improve it. Reagan got the MX missile, the improved Trident D-5 missile for submarines, and the B-1 and Stealth bombers in his budget and at least partially funded by the end of 1981. In March 1983, he started the Strategic Defense Initiative—a program of unknown outcome at the time but also one that the Soviets had no way to counter. In late 1983, following persistent efforts to work with US allies in NATO, the Pershing II and cruise missiles were introduced into Western Europe to counter the threat of Soviet missiles aimed at cities there. The Pershing IIs frightened the Soviets. "They are a gun to our temple," Gorbachev would tell his advisors.

With all that in place, Reagan persuaded the Soviet leaders that a nuclear war would be a disaster for them as well as the United States and Europe. Once they were convinced, the decline in the Soviet arsenals was as systematic as the buildup had been.

Reagan's ultimate goal—"the dream," he called it—was the complete elimination of nuclear weapons and much greater reliance on anti-missile defense than on retaliation for a missile attack. Reagan actually offered to share a missile defense system, if an effective technology were developed, with the Soviets and the rest of the world. In the meantime, he focused immediate efforts on ensuring the effectiveness of the US nuclear deterrent. The MX itself was partly designed to make the Soviet leaders realize—which they hadn't until then—that the weapon, given its power and precision, assured their personal demise in a nuclear war.

Reagan's strategy, well established in his first year in office, did not change: it was to make absolutely sure in the minds of the Soviets that they faced destruction in a nuclear war. Thus they, too, adopted—at Geneva and in individual statements—the view that a nuclear war could not be won and must never be fought. The evolution of their view occurred as Reagan sought an alternative through strategic defense to make nuclear missiles obsolete and thus eliminate the possibility of an all-out nuclear war.

Reagan, in short, left the world a safer place.

CHAPTER THREE

If the Soviets Attacked

If the Soviet Union were to attack the United States in an all-out nuclear war, 150 million US residents—roughly three Americans out of five—would be killed. That estimate was delivered to President Reagan at the December 3, 1981, classified meeting of the National Security Council (NSC).[1]

Reagan had been aware of the horrors of nuclear war for decades—from the time he heard about the bombings of Hiroshima and Nagasaki that ended World War II. But this was an estimate from his own experts—the Joint Chiefs of Staff who are the military advisors to the NSC—of the consequences in the 1980s of an all-out Soviet first strike. And 150 million deaths would only be the immediate impact. A great many other people would die from radiation, starvation, and the absence of medical care.

By comparison, a comparable attack in 2011, when the US population numbered 312 million, would kill closer to 218 million people then residing in the United States—or perhaps even more, because of greater concentration of the population in urban centers.

Reagan was wrestling with the question whether it was worthwhile to greatly increase the country's expenditures on civil defense. Civil defense was, as pointed out in the meeting, one of the components of the president's strategic-force modernization plans. Everyone agreed that civil defense was important: a more vulnerable America was a more tempting target for the Soviets.

Under consideration that day in 1981 were three options for civil defense. Option 1 did not involve any substantial budget increases. Option 2 increased the means of protecting the population, primarily by shelters; but it postponed for a year a decision on industrial protection and blast shelters. Option 3 included industrial protection for defense industries and industries critical to supporting the population, as well as blast shelters for key workers. It involved a commitment of $7.3 billion over five years—funds that would probably come, in the end, from the defense budget.

"Both Options 2 and 3 require investment of some $237 million in FY 83," Reagan noted. "There is no question in my mind that the Soviet Union has a tremendous advantage in civil defense just as it has an advantage in weapons," he continued. "It's obvious that no one wants Option 1. . . . Option 2 does not yet commit us to the most expensive program. It is a shame that we do not have extensive caves near our population centers."[2] He pointed out that the Soviets already had underground factories.

As the discussion went back and forth, Reagan asked whether evacuation of cities was practical.

That's when Reagan got the casualty estimate of 150 million people. Admiral James Nance said that "JCS estimates that if the Soviets evacuate their cities prior to a nuclear attack, their losses would be 15 million, a number less than they lost in the Second World War or in the purges. The US, on the other hand, would lose some 150 million people."[3]

Reagan asked how we would care for all the evacuees who left high-risk areas. He got only a statement from General Lewis of the Federal Emergency Management Agency that we could "beef up the host areas;" and in any case people wouldn't have to stay very long— nature would take care of radiation, and decontamination operations would be conducted.

Reagan wasn't convinced. He approved an increase in civil defense expenditures at the December 3 meeting, but he chose Option 2—a moderate increase rather than the all-out effort Option 3 would have involved. He had learned at the meeting that US cities really couldn't be effectively evacuated and their populations protected and taken care of, even with Option 3.

Reagan never used the estimate of 150 million deaths from a Soviet nuclear attack in a speech, in any comments to reporters, or even in his presidential memoirs. He noted it only in his personal diary, first published in 2007 (the unabridged diary came out in 2009). On the night of December 3, 1981, he wrote:

> N.S.C. meeting—I approved starting a Civil Defense buildup. Right now in a nuclear war we'd lose 150 mil. people. The Soviets could hold their loss down to less than were killed in W.W. II.[4]

Less than two weeks later, Reagan heard from the Vatican. At the request of Pope John Paul II, he met with a papal delegation of scholars who were delivering a report on nuclear war prepared by fourteen scientists under the auspices of the Pontifical Academy of Sciences. The delegation visiting Reagan included four American professors: Victor F. Weisskopf and David Baltimore of MIT, Howard H. Hiatt, dean of the Harvard School of Public Health, and Marshall W. Nirenberg of the National Institutes of Health. The delegation's report stated that:

> The conditions of life following a nuclear attack would be so severe that the only hope for humanity is prevention of any form of nuclear war. . . [which] would inevitably cause death, disease and suffering of pandemic proportions and without the possibility of effective medical intervention. . . . It should be noted that the bomb dropped on Nagasaki had a power of about 20,000 tons of TNT, not much larger than the so-called 'tactical bombs' designed for battlefield use.
>
> The suffering of the surviving population would be without parallel. There would be complete interruption of communications, of food supplies and of water. Help would be given only at the risk of mortal danger from radiation for those venturing outside of buildings in the first days. The social disruption following such an attack would be unimaginable. . . . Even a nuclear attack directed only at military facilities would be devastating to the country as a whole. . . . An objective

examination of the medical situation that would follow a nuclear war leads to but one conclusion: prevention is our only recourse.[5]

The meeting was brief—20 minutes—but impressive enough that Reagan recorded it in his diary, summarizing with his usual skill at getting to the essence: " . . . meeting with 4 professors—the Pope's Vatican study team on Nuclear War. Their findings—we must not have one."[6]

The four professors were not sure what effect they had on the president. But the next day—discussing the report with the Pope's secretary of state, Cardinal Casaroli—Reagan noted that he "was struck by the . . . conclusion that in the event of a war there would be no way to care for the huge numbers of wounded."[7]

Reagan's abhorrence of war, especially nuclear war, was so great that some of his advisors believed he would not have retaliated against a Soviet first strike. For example, Jack Matlock, Reagan's NSC advisor on Soviet affairs and later his ambassador to the Soviet Union, said in an interview in 2001 that he "sensed" that Reagan could not bring himself to strike another country with nuclear weapons.[8] But Reagan's own writings and interviews demonstrate that this judgment about him is simply wrong.

In an interview on January 9, 1989[9]—just before he left the presidency—Reagan recalled a remark made by former President Lyndon Johnson at a Nixon state dinner[10] held in California. Reagan, who was then governor of California, remembered the conversation as follows:

> He [Johnson] made a remark I never forgot and I didn't understand really how anyone could think of this job and make such a remark. He said that when Richard Nixon took the oath [to become president] "the greatest burden lifted from me that I have ever carried in my life." He said, "I never—there was never a day went by that I wasn't frightened or scared that I might be the man that started World War III."

Well how can you be scared of such—as if that's something that comes on you and you don't have anything to do with it? And if such a war became necessary—as it always has been in our country, we've never started the wars, how could you—you'd have to accept it. That's part of what this job is all about . . . how could he sit there living in fear that somehow he might trigger a war?

. . . You know that there could be one but I would know also we wouldn't start it . . . It would be forced upon us. . . .

Reagan went on to note that, in his view, the greatest threat to war was "the manner in which our military had been allowed to deteriorate." Strength was the ultimate deterrent.

The Anderson Interview

On July 25, 1989, Martin Anderson met with Ronald Reagan in Los Angeles. Anderson was interviewing Reagan for an update to Anderson's book *Revolution*, which had been published the previous year.[11] Reagan had recently left the presidency, and was reflecting on the policies of his eight years in office. He was open and ready to talk, and spoke at length about his responsibilities as president and the decisions he might have had to make about nuclear war.

Anderson opened the interview by asking whether Reagan had gotten done what he wanted to do. Reagan replied that although he didn't accomplish everything, he had a plan.

Anderson: A little over ten years ago, I went with you to the ranch in Santa Barbara. You had an interview with Bill Moyers, and he challenged you then. I remember him saying—this was when you were just thinking about running for president, in 1979—"You know some people will say you're too old, you're too reluctant, you're not hungry enough to pay the price of becoming president, and you're out of touch." You said, "Well, I don't want to be president in the sense that I want to live in the White House, but I want, I want the chance . . . there are things that I think can be done." But now looking back, ten years later, did you get done some of the big things you wanted to get done?

Reagan: Oh, yes. Didn't get them all, there's some things that really haunt me to this day and I'll sit around the mashed potato circuit and they'll find out up at the [Bohemian] Grove[12] Saturday I'm still talking about it.

But when I think back, the one thing as I look back and think maybe was different from many who have taken that position was I had a plan, I had a program. I really was, as I said there, concerned about something that I thought had to happen in government.

We were coming into a time when America was being told, even by its leaders then, to lower their sights, that never again would we have the lush days that we'd had. We found out that on any given day 50 percent of our military aircraft couldn't fly for lack of spare parts and our ships couldn't leave harbor for that or lack of crew. We had the double-digit inflation, we had the double-digit unemployment, and we were really in economic recession, which we were being told was really what we must get used to, that this was going to be—likely to be—the way things were, you know.

I had some strong beliefs.

Anderson and Reagan talked about the books already published about the Reagan administration that painted Reagan as not accomplishing much and, in any case, having nothing to do with whatever *was* accomplished. Reagan found this almost unbelievable. They also talked about the role of Reagan's vice president, George H. W. Bush, whether Reagan had second thoughts about not firing Office of Management and Budget Director David Stockman, and even the US action in Grenada.

After a time, they turned again to the nuclear situation:

Anderson: Let me go back to that plan [you mentioned], because I think that when the historians look back at these eight years they may say that the most important thing you achieved was nuclear disarmament with the Soviet Union.

And I remember back in 1976, at the convention in Kansas City, when President Ford called you down, waved you down from up in the balcony. And you made a speech that night, it was off the cuff, extemporaneous . . . You talked about the great challenge we face, and that challenge, you said, was that we lived in a world in which the great powers have poised, aimed at each other, the horrible missiles of destruction that can in a matter of minutes arrive in each other's country and virtually destroy the civilized world we live in.

It seems to me that over the past thirteen years you have continually come back to that theme—what can we do about reducing the threat of nuclear war. I just wonder, did you have a plan all along? Was the defense buildup tied to that? Was SDI [the Strategic Defense Initiative] tied to that? In other words, were the defense buildup and SDI part of the plan to do something about nuclear war, or were they separate?

Reagan: No, they were together. First of all, we inherited the Mutual Assured Destruction, the MAD, policy. I thought that was the most ridiculous thing I had ever seen, that you could stand there, like two guys with guns pointed at each other's heads and cocked and thinking that neither one of them will take a chance and pull on that trigger. But to have the power to destroy, literally, the civilized world, and it would only take somebody pushing a button to launch that, because if they launched theirs first, you know that ours would be on their way even though we'd be blown up, too.

This was the first time in the interview that Reagan explicitly stated that if the Soviets attacked, the United States would retaliate. The alternative to MAD was strategic defense. Reagan went on to talk about the steps he took that led to the SDI:

Reagan: So one of the early things I did was that I called a meeting of the chiefs of staff in the cabinet room. And I said, look, every weapon that's ever been created in the world has resulted in a defense, a defensive weapon, the sword and later the shield, and so forth. And I said, isn't it with our technology possible that we could produce a system that could hit those missiles as they came out of their silos, using space, whatever? Well, they kind of huddled for a minute, and then they came back and they said could you give us a couple of days on that? And I said yes.

In a couple of days they came back. And they said, yes, we think it is worthwhile. We think with today's technology we can develop something of that kind that would virtually make them obsolete. Because no one would want to press the button if you knew that only a half a dozen of the weapons would ever get through, leaving us able then to retaliate. So I said, all right, we start, go to it. And so we started that plan.

Reagan continued with a description of his negotiations with Soviet President Mikhail Gorbachev, and the centrality of the Strategic Defense Initiative:

Reagan: And to the point that at my first meeting with Gorbachev he jumped on that. And I said, that is not a bargaining chip. And I told him, I said, look, if we're successful with that, what we're doing, I'll tell you what my own view is, we should share it with you and with the world. Because all of us know how to make those missiles now, so if we do just say we're going to eliminate them, and we eliminate them, we would still have to live with the thought that someday along could come a man like Hitler and make them again, and blackmail the world. So I said this is like we did back in 1925 when we all met in Switzerland and decided against chemical warfare. And I said we all agreed to do away with them, and we all kept our gas masks.

Anderson: Did he agree with your basic thrust?

Reagan: For one thing, he said, "I don't believe you"—[that is,] that I would share.

So what is obvious, what his attempt was, and several times later he did it, his attempt was I think to find some way to get—by reducing arms and everything—to get us to give up on it. But I've also suspected, and I think there's evidence to bear this out, that the Soviet Union scientists were exploring the same thing, only they don't have our technology yet and couldn't do it.

I spoke a line, when I addressed the British Parliament and I think to some other government bodies in other countries: "A nuclear war cannot be won and must never be fought." And the biggest thrill I had was in a meeting a few years later than that in our country, when Mr. Gorbachev's foreign secretary, Shevardnadze, speaking on his own, said "a nuclear war can never be won and must never be fought."

Anderson: Good line.

Reagan: But the thing was, I guess I got sidetracked here also, my plan was that in the past with our summit meetings with the Soviets and their leaders and all, we were always trying to get some agreement out of them by making concessions, and I came in determined that the only way to peace was through strength.

When I called them the Evil Empire in a public speech, I did it on purpose. I wanted them to know that we saw them for what they were, and as I said to him at one meeting, one of our earliest meetings, to Gorbachev, I told him it was someone else's line that we didn't mistrust each other because we were armed, but [were] armed because we mistrusted each other.

Even at the time of Martin Anderson's interview—in 1989—the view was emerging that Reagan had changed his policies toward the Soviets in his second term. Anderson asked him about this.

Anderson: Some of my conservative friends think that you flip flopped and changed your mind—that at one point you called them the Evil Empire and the next thing you know, you were dealing with them and negotiating with them. . . . And I tried to explain, I think you had something else in mind.

Reagan: Yes, because I said to him then, after I said that, I said "it's not enough, you and I, engaged in dealings here trying to reduce the weaponry that we have, why don't we start trying to reduce what causes the mistrust between us. But I will tell you now, we can continue to disarm or we can continue the arms race, and I'll tell you now, you can't win the arms race. There is no way."

Reagan: He is the first Russian leader since the Revolution who has ever agreed to a treaty in which they would destroy weapons they already have, the INF [Intermediate-Range Nuclear Forces] treaty. Always before, they would make treaties about how many they would come to, but never were they willing to destroy a weapon. And now you hear him offering to destroy them all.

Anderson: Well, he's smarter than I thought he was.

Reagan: And I made it plain to him also that in the destroying of nuclear weapons, this was going to have to be tied to the conventional, because they had superiority and the only thing we had to respond to that superiority was nuclear. So we weren't going to sit here and join them in a nuclear disarmament at the expense of leaving them with a 10 to 1 advantage in tanks and artillery.

Anderson delved further into Reagan's policies on nuclear strategy—what Reagan would do in the event of a nuclear attack.

Anderson: I don't know if anyone has ever asked you this, but I've often wondered: it seemed to me that probably the toughest thing about being president was that you had the responsibility of ultimately deciding whether or not to retaliate in case the Soviets attacked us. How did you think about that? Did you have any contingency plan? Did you ever think and say, my God, what if they do? You know, what will we do? Will we just sit here and accept the missiles; will we launch a retaliatory attack? How did you deal with that?

Reagan: One of the difficulties in bargaining with them was most of their nuclear force was land based, missiles in silos. Ours was a triad—missiles in silos, nuclear submarines, and so forth out there and with weapons that had to be tracked down in the ocean and they could hit Russian targets, and an air force that could fly them. So that in order for them to be safe, it wasn't good enough to just destroy the missiles in the silos here—

But, yes, our reply, and I had to—and this had to be—that if ever the word came, that they had pushed the button, yes, we had to set all of ours in motion.

For the second time in the interview, Reagan calmly stated that "This had to be"—the United States would retaliate against a Soviet first strike. Anderson went on to ask whether Reagan thought that "the Soviets understood this clearly?"

Reagan: I have a hunch they did, yes, because I made it very plain to him—what we were gonna take and what we weren't going to take.

Because Washington was a top target of Soviet planners and their nuclear submarines were often cruising the Western Atlantic, Reagan also knew, as he recorded in his autobiography, that he himself would almost surely be killed within several minutes after a Soviet launch. One of Reagan's major decisions—to pursue the MX missile, with its extremely accurate targeting capabilities—was to convince the Soviet leaders that they themselves—personally—were as vulnerable as US leaders.

Reagan wrote to Anderson on June 18, 1990, requesting that the interview statements on nuclear retaliation not be quoted during his lifetime, concerned that even then his words would be misused:

"While I certainly was prepared to respond appropriately to any attack on our country, I am sure you can understand the implications of being reported as willing to 'push the button.' I guess it's one of those things that are understood, but better left unsaid. I'm just afraid our opponents could have a heyday with that."

———————

From the moment he took office until he left, President Reagan was sharply aware of the threat of nuclear war and of the responsibilities and decisions he would face as president. He wrote about it not long after leaving office, in his autobiographical memoir, *An American Life:*[13]

> As president, I carried no wallet, no money, no driver's license, no keys in my pocket—only secret codes that were capable of bringing about the annihilation of much of the world as we knew it.
>
> On inauguration day, after being briefed a few days earlier on what I was to do if ever it became necessary to unleash American nuclear weapons, I'd taken over the greatest responsibility of my life—of any human being's life.
>
> From then on, wherever I went, I carried a small plastic-coated card with me, and a military aide with a very special job was always close by. He or she (I was pleased to be able to appoint the first female officer to this position) carried a small bag everyone referred to as 'the football.' It contained the directives for launching our nuclear weapons in retaliation for a nuclear attack on our country.
>
> The plastic-coated card, which I carried in a small pocket in my coat, listed the codes I would issue to the Pentagon confirming that it was actually the president of the United States who was ordering the unleashing of our nuclear weapons.
>
> The decision to launch the weapon was mine alone to make.
>
> We had many contingency plans for responding to a nuclear attack. But everything would happen so fast that I wondered how much planning or reason could be applied in such a crisis. The Russians sometimes kept submarines off our East Coast with nuclear missiles that

could turn the White House into a pile of radioactive rubble within six or eight minutes.

Six minutes to decide how to respond to a blip on a radar scope and decide whether to unleash Armageddon!

How could anyone apply reason at a time like that?

There were some people in the Pentagon who thought in terms of fighting and *winning* a nuclear war. To me it was simple common sense: A nuclear war couldn't be won by either side. It must never be fought. But how do we go about trying to prevent it and pulling back from this hair-trigger existence?

CHAPTER FOUR

Development of the Nuclear Arsenals

Ronald Reagan was not the only president to ponder the problem of a Soviet nuclear attack. This chapter looks at the development of the US and Soviet nuclear arsenals, displayed on the graph in this chapter, from the Truman administration through the Reagan administration, in the following sections:

The Truman Years: 1945–53
The Eisenhower Buildup: 1953–61
JFK: The Buildup Continues: 1961–63
Lyndon Baines Johnson: The First Decline: 1963–69
Richard Nixon and Missile Defense: 1969–74
Gerald R. Ford: The Second Decline: 1974–77
The Carter Crossover: 1977–81
Ronald Reagan and the Soviet Reversal: 1981–89

Because mutual assured destruction has been such a central feature of nuclear strategy, we give each president's public statements about it explicit attention. At the same time, we recount what Reagan was doing as other presidents dealt with the nuclear threat.

The Truman Years: 1945–53

While President Harry Truman and British Prime Minister Winston Churchill were making the decision to use the atomic bomb on Japan, Ronald Reagan was on duty in the US military, serving in the First Motion Picture Unit of the Army Air Corps. His tasks included narrating the Tokyo "target films" made for the pilots who were drop-ping bombs on Japanese targets. The First Motion Picture Unit built realistic models that they kept updated. The films, including specific targeting information, were shipped to the Far East, where the pilots viewed them before taking off on their bombing runs.

By the time Reagan was called up for military service in 1942, he was already an accomplished actor. Since June 1, 1937, he had made thirty feature films under contract to Warner Bros. His poor vision precluded front-line service, but he entered the Army as a second lieutenant. He had joined a reserve cavalry unit while working as a sportscaster in Des Moines, Iowa. Before he left for Hollywood, he completed the courses and exams to become a reserve office. During the war, the Army loaned him to Warner Bros. to make the top box-office movie of 1943, "This Is the Army."[1]

The first atomic bomb was exploded over Hiroshima on August 6, 1945. It used uranium. The second bomb, detonated over Nagasaki on August 9, 1945, used plutonium. One bomb had been detonated in the Trinity test in New Mexico on July 16, 1945. With those three atomic weapons exploded, only one remained in the US arsenal.

The United States was then the world's sole nuclear power, but physicists around the world understood the concept of nuclear reac-tions. President Truman presented a proposal to turn atomic weapons over to an international agency—provided other countries agreed not to produce them; the agency would also control peaceful uses of atomic energy. The Soviets refused. With its scientists aided by Soviet spies in the US nuclear establishment, the Soviet Union tested its first bomb in 1949. By the time Truman left office, the Soviets had fifty nuclear weapons, the United States 841.[2]

Besides building atomic bombs, Truman gave the go-ahead in 1950 to develop the far more powerful hydrogen bomb, which was suc-cessfully tested in 1952. The Soviets were not far behind, testing their hydrogen bomb in 1955.

By the end of the war, Reagan was a captain in the Army Air Corps and the adjutant of the First Motion Picture Unit. He was released from service in December 1945. Not long afterward, he did a dramatic

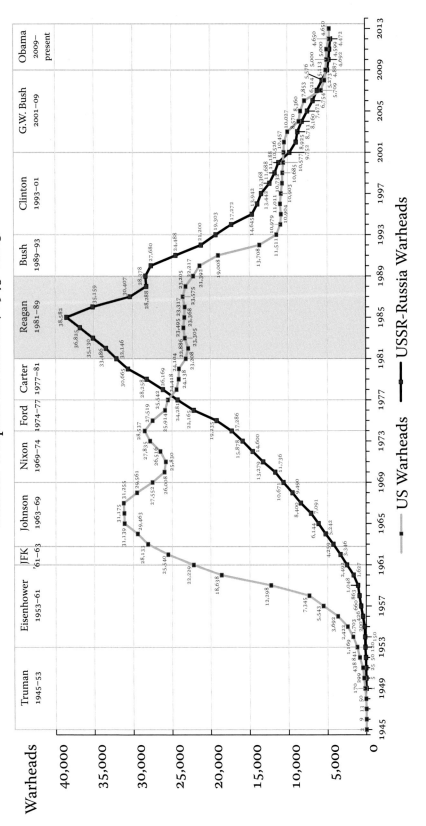

Nuclear Weapons Inventories, 1945–2013

reading of Norman Corwin's anti-nuclear poem, "Set Your Clock at U-235," but Warner Bros. forbade further readings on the grounds that it violated his contract—the reading was "a performance."

Reagan returned to his acting career, and was elected by his peers president of the Screen Actors Guild. He served altogether seven terms, negotiating with all kinds of tough adversaries, from communists to studio heads. In 1947, he testified, at Richard Nixon's request, before the House Un-American Activities Committee on communist influence in the motion picture industry. Reagan "named no names," in the popular phrase of that time. He stated that in the Screen Actors Guild, of which he was president, a small clique was "suspected of more or less following the tactics that we associate with the Communist Party."[3] He went on to emphasize that the guild had been successful, using democratic procedures, at exposing their lies and opposing their propaganda: "I do not believe the communists have ever at any time been able to use the motion picture screen as a sounding board for their philosophy or ideology. . . . I would hesitate to see any political party outlawed on the basis of its political ideology. . . . I still think that democracy can do it."[4]

Reagan reflected on the immediate post-war era in a May 1979 radio commentary:

Of course, the Cold War, the subversion and attempts at infiltration were very real and very much part of an overall Communist plan. In Hollywood in 1947, when several Communist-infiltrated unions attacked their fellow workers by way of a jurisdictional strike, when there was physical violence and bombings, it was all very real. I was part of that Hollywood and participated in the successful effort to keep the studios open and operating.

Today all of those stormy years are lumped together by the history re-writers and laid on the doorstep of the late Senator McCarthy. Indeed, the term "McCarthyism" is used to identify that entire era. Actually, the senator didn't make his charges and begin his investigations until several years after the Communist effort in Hollywood had been defeated. But it's true that the senator used a shotgun when a rifle was needed, injuring the innocent along with the guilty. Nevertheless, his broadsides should not be used today to infer that all who opposed Communist subversion were hysterical zealots while the Communists were high-minded liberals, free thinkers, and not really Communists at all.[5]

In the broader political realm, Reagan campaigned for Truman's re-election in 1948.

The Eisenhower Buildup: 1953–61

The most stunning characteristic of the Eisenhower years is the buildup of nuclear weapons. At the end of 1952, Truman's last full year in office, the United States had 851 warheads—mostly atomic bombs. The Soviet Union—which had built its first bomb in 1949—had fifty.

Reagan signed a letter supporting Eisenhower for president in the 1952 election, assuming Ike would be running as a Democrat. When Ike decided to run as a Republican, Reagan decided to continue to support him, and did so again in 1956.

In his famous "Atoms for Peace" speech, in December 1953, Eisenhower reviewed the horrors of atomic warfare and laid out a US response to a nuclear attack:

> Should such an atomic attack be launched against the United States, our reactions would be swift and resolute. But for me to say that the defense capabilities of the United States are such that they could inflict terrible losses upon an aggressor—for me to say that the retaliation capabilities of the United States are so great that such an aggressor's land would be laid waste—all this, while fact, is not the true expression of the purpose and the hope of the United States.[6]

Having made clear the threat, Eisenhower went on to explain that the real purpose was, rather, to make atomic energy available for peaceful purposes: "To the making of these fateful decisions, the United States pledges before you . . . its determination to help solve the fearful atomic dilemma—to devote its entire heart and mind to find the way by which the miraculous inventiveness of man shall not be dedicated to his death, but consecrated to his life."[7]

Years later—exactly thirty years to the day—President Reagan would quote this part of the speech to the Washington press corps from a 3 × 5 card he kept in his desk. He had written the quotation in his own hand.

By the end of 1953, the Soviets had added another seventy bombs to their arsenal. On July 28, 1955, Eisenhower was briefed on the capability of developing nuclear-tipped intercontinental ballistic missiles, and the likely Soviet effort underway to do so as well. Ike signed a National Security Council action document to proceed on the "highest priority" September 13, 1955.[8] On October 4, 1957, the Soviets launched an earth-orbiting satellite known as Sputnik. Sputnik II, with a dog on board, was launched a month later (the dog died). The Soviets were testing their missiles.

In his news conference on August 27, 1958, Eisenhower was asked whether the United States had to take the "first blow" in a nuclear war. The questioner, reporter May Craig, noted that Congress was so hostile to any discussion of a possible surrender by the United States in a nuclear war that they had forbidden spending any military money to study the possibility. "Is it your position that we must take the first blow?" she asked.

Eisenhower replied that "wars have a way of coming about in circumstances that have not been foreseen by humans." He noted that the attack on Pearl Harbor by the Japanese was a case in point: "Of all the places in the Pacific that apparently the planners and the political leaders thought might be attacked, that was probably the last one."

Eisenhower was making the point that we could be surprised by an attack. But he reversed himself virtually immediately and went on to say that we couldn't be defeated in a first strike because no nation would be so foolish as to do such a thing: "I don't see any reason, therefore, for saying we necessarily have to take the first blow. But I do say this: always we must be alert. And I think it is silly to say that we can be defeated in a first-blow attack, for the simple reason that we have so much strength, retaliatory strength, that any nation foolish [enough] to resort to that kind of an effort—that is, the exchange of nuclear attacks—would itself be destroyed. There is no question in my mind."[9]

Eisenhower had reason to be certain. By the end of 1958, the United States would have 7,345 nuclear weapons to the Soviets' 863,[10] an 8 to 1 ratio. Most of the weapons were bombs to be dropped by aircraft. The Soviets already had a few sea-launched ballistic missiles; the intercontinental ballistic missile (ICBM) was on the drawing boards, but as Ike said later in the news conference, "There is still a long way to go before the airplane, I would say, is made completely obsolete."[11]

During his two terms in office, Eisenhower had increased the nuclear arsenal of the United States to 18,638 warheads, a far greater stockpile than the Soviets' 1,627.[12]

The Republican Party nominated Richard Nixon, Eisenhower's vice president, as its 1960 presidential candidate to succeed Eisenhower. Nixon lost the 1960 election to John Fitzgerald Kennedy. Reagan had been asked by Joseph P. Kennedy to support JFK, but Reagan— although still a Democrat—supported Nixon.

Reagan's presence on the silver screen faded gradually in the 1950s. He made twenty-two feature films after the war, the last in 1964. But his appearances as a television actor increased. His first role on television was in 1950 on an episode of Nash Airflyte Theatre's anthology, in which he played a detective. In 1952, he married Nancy Davis. He did a stint in Las Vegas as an opener for a night-club act; it was a way to put bread on the table. Nancy went with him.

In 1954, Reagan was chosen by General Electric to be the unifying figure for its Sunday television series, "General Electric Theater," a popular television drama. He acted in several episodes. His job with GE included visiting its plants around the country, speaking to employees and conducting question-and-answer sessions with them. On these tours—two a year of several weeks each—he also spoke to civic groups. In fact, he became one of the most sought-after speakers in the country. He spoke increasingly about high taxes, the influence of the bureaucracy and regulation, and other problems he believed stemmed from the size of the federal government.

Richard Nixon wrote to Reagan in 1959 to compliment him on one of these speeches, beginning a correspondence between the two of them that would continue until Nixon's death in 1994. Speaking as a Democrat for Nixon was a natural fit.[13]

JFK: The Buildup Continues: 1961–63

In the first year of his presidency—on November 2, 1961—President John F. Kennedy issued a statement on nuclear tests being conducted by the Soviet Union. He discounted the idea that the Soviet tests were "bluff and bluster," but he did take the occasion to affirm US strength and willingness to retaliate: "The United States does not find it necessary to explode 50-megaton nuclear devices to confirm that we have many times more nuclear power than any other nation on earth and that these capabilities are deployed so as to survive any sneak attack and thus enable us to devastate any nation which initiates a nuclear attack on the United States or its Allies. It is essential to the defense of the Free World that we maintain this relative position."[14]

When Kennedy made this statement, the United States was ahead of the Soviets in ICBMs, sea-launched ballistic missiles, and vastly ahead in bombers. The total warheads were United States, 22,229; Soviets, 2,492. The ratio was almost 9 to 1,[15] thanks to dramatic additions to the nuclear triad—bombers, submarines, and ICBMs—made under Eisenhower.

Meanwhile, the Soviets were also building nuclear weapons—one hundred a year, then two hundred, then six hundred. The weapons test that prompted Kennedy's statement occurred on October 30, 1961 over the Novaya Zemlya archipelago in the Arctic north of the Soviet mainland, and was the most powerful nuclear weapon ever detonated. It was part of a series of nuclear weapons tests begun on September 1, 1961, two months earlier, and continuing through 1962.

The Soviets challenged Kennedy in other ways. The Berlin Wall was built (beginning on August 13, 1961) by the East Germans during the Kennedy administration. Kennedy also experienced the failure of the Bay of Pigs invasion of Cuba in April 1961 and the Cuban missile crisis in October 1962, a confrontation that brought the world as close to nuclear war as it came during the Cold War.

In April 1962, General Electric cancelled "General Electric Theater." Ronald Reagan was out of a job. He had written a letter to GE on January 30, 1961—over a year before the cancellation—warning them that if they cut the budget for the program as they were proposing to do, it would fail: fewer guest stars would be hired, and fewer new shows would be produced. GE officials claimed they cancelled the show because the competition from "Bonanza," which moved from Saturday night to Sunday opposite "General Electric Theater," damaged the program's ratings. Reagan was convinced that GE was also under political pressure from the Kennedy administration because of Reagan's outspoken speeches on the GE tour.

Within a few months after the cancellation, publisher Duell, Sloan and Pearce expressed interest in a book about Reagan's own life. By September 1962, he and a co-author, Richard Hubler, had a contract for the book. Reagan would go on to host "Death Valley Days" on television. He made one last movie, but he was gradually shifting from entertainment to politics, campaigning for Richard Nixon for governor of California in 1962. In the fall of that year, Reagan formally switched his political registration from Democrat to Republican.

Lyndon Baines Johnson: The First Decline: 1963–69

Lyndon Baines Johnson became president on November 22, 1963, when Kennedy was assassinated. Johnson then won the 1964 election, defeating Barry Goldwater. On October 27, 1964, Ronald Reagan gave the televised speech in support of Goldwater that is considered to be his debut on the political scene.

President Johnson, commissioning the 28th nuclear-powered Polaris submarine, the USS *Sam Rayburn*, on December 2, 1964, noted that "the purpose of this new submarine—like those which came before—is not war, but peace. While such power exists, no potential enemy can hope to profit from an unprovoked, surprise attack on the United States. Our Polaris missiles, together with our strategic bombers and our long-range missiles ashore, guarantee any adversary that retaliation for a nuclear attack on this country would be inevitable and devastating."[16]

The United States was ahead of the Soviets in all parts of the strategic triad at the end of 1964, with total warheads at 29,463 for the United States and 5,242 for the Soviets.[17] But the ratio was now less than 6 to 1. The Soviets were building. And they kept on building, especially the intercontinental ballistic missiles that could strike the United States.

After the cancellation of "General Electric Theater," Reagan increased his participation in Republican politics and campaigned for Barry Goldwater in 1964, making his famous pro-Goldwater television speech on October 27, 1964. The speech—based in large part on what Reagan had been saying to civic groups for years—was so effective that when Goldwater lost to Johnson in November of 1964, Reagan immediately emerged as a possible nominee of the Republican Party in 1968 and, more realistically, as a candidate for California governor.

Reagan's first autobiography, *Where's the Rest of Me?*, was published in April 1965. In November 1966, during Johnson's second term in office, he was elected governor of California. On September 28, 1967, he made a speech at his alma mater, Eureka College in Eureka, Illinois, in which he said, "We are the generation that exploded the atomic bomb and brought a permanent terror to the world."[18]

As the chart shows, the US arsenal reached a peak in 1967 at 31,255 warheads. It leveled off in Johnson's later years and then started its decline. Johnson decided not to run in 1968, his public support severely eroded by the war in Vietnam. In that election, Nixon beat Hubert H. Humphrey, Johnson's vice president. As Johnson turned the presidency over to Richard Nixon, the United States had 29,561 warheads to the Soviets' 9,490.[19] It was apparent that only the Soviets were building.

Richard Nixon and Missile Defense: 1969–74

On February 18, 1970, President Richard Nixon delivered his first annual report to Congress on US foreign policy for the 1970s in which he said that ". . . the overriding purpose of our strategic posture is political and defensive: to deny other countries the ability to impose their will on the United States and its allies under the weight of military superiority. We must insure that all potential aggressors see unacceptable risks in contemplating a nuclear attack, or nuclear blackmail, or acts which could escalate to strategic nuclear war, such as a Soviet conventional attack on Europe."[20]

As the report pointed out, the Soviets were continuing to build: "The Soviets' present build-up of strategic forces, together with what we know about their development and test programs, raises serious questions about where they are headed and the potential threats we and our allies face."[21] By the end of 1970, the Soviets had 11,736 nuclear warheads; the United States had 26,008.[22] The ratio was down to just over 2 to 1.

Nixon made a major decision: to continue constructing the Safeguard anti-ballistic missile system. That, he said, was consistent with the purpose of deterring aggression and with the goal of effective arms control. Nixon recalled his March 1969 statement on missile defense, in which he said:

". . . [W]e cannot ignore the potential Chinese threat against the US population, as well as the danger of an accidental or unauthorized attack from any source. Nor can we dismiss the possibility that other countries may in the future acquire the capability to attack the US with nuclear weapons. Today, any nuclear attack—no matter how small; whether accidental, unauthorized or by designs; by a superpower or by a country with only a primitive nuclear delivery capability—would be a catastrophe for the US, no matter how devastating our ability to retaliate. No administration with the responsibility for the lives and security of the American people could fail to provide every possible protection against such eventualities."[23,24]

The anti-ballistic missile (ABM) system was a hard sell. Vice President Spiro Agnew broke a tie in the Senate on August 6, 1969, to ensure funding for two ABM sites, later cut back to one. Originally, ten or more had been planned, to protect cities as well as missile fields. Then Nixon negotiated the ABM treaty with the Soviets. Signed in 1972, it limited defensive sites—first to two, then to one. The site at Grand Forks, North Dakota, which held one hundred defensive missiles to deal with an incoming attack, became operational in part in April 1975, during the Ford administration, and fully operational on October 1, 1975. The next day, Congress voted to withdraw funds and shut down the radar that enabled the site to identify incoming missiles.

During Nixon's presidency, the number of ICBMs and sea-launched missiles grew; warheads on bombers stayed about the same. Nixon increased the nuclear arsenal to 28,537 warheads. But the Soviets were building faster—at the rate of about 1,500 a year; by the end of 1974, they had 17,286, reducing the US advantage to less than 2 to 1.[25] The US nuclear arsenal declined when Nixon lost power, and continued to decline under presidents Ford and Carter.

Besides Nixon's pursuit of missile defense, three of his accomplishments stand out: the end of the Vietnam War, the establishment of an all-volunteer armed force, and the opening to China. The number of US military troops in Vietnam declined from the peak of over half a million in 1968 to just over 24,000 in 1972.[26] Nixon supported the goal of an all-volunteer armed force in public, beginning with a campaign statement in 1967. A White House commission to study the possibility reported in February 1970. Draft calls steadily decreased, reaching zero in January 1973; in June 1973, authority to the executive branch to draft, renewed every two years, simply expired.[27]

Ronald Reagan was the governor of California during the entire Nixon presidency; he was elected two years before Nixon was elected president, and was in his second term when Nixon resigned. He supported Nixon throughout, including the latter's efforts to end the Vietnam War and abolish the draft. He explained his long-time support of the US involvement in Vietnam War in a January 15, 1980 letter: "I supported the mining of Haiphong Harbor and the bombing of Hanoi [in 1972] enthusiastically and was, indeed, considered a hawk because I have continued to say that the only immorality of the Vietnam War was that our government asked young men to die in a war that the government had no intention of winning."[28] In the domestic policy area, Reagan testified against Nixon's Family Assistance Plan, which was ultimately defeated.

Journalist/author Lou Cannon would sum up Reagan's eight years as governor by noting that "Reagan had more impact on the domestic policies of the Nixon administration than any other governor, and his welfare policies are now widely copied by other states."[29]

Reagan made four international goodwill trips at Nixon's request, three to Asia and one to Europe, carrying personal messages from the president to foreign leaders. In 1969, he went to the Philippines, stopping over in Hong Kong; in 1971, to Taiwan, Japan, South Korea, Singapore, Thailand, and South Vietnam. The Taiwan visit was especially important. Its goal was to reassure Chiang Kai-shek of US support at a time when Henry Kissinger was preparing to visit the People's Republic of China. In 1972, at Nixon's request, Reagan met in Brussels with the heads of six European nations and NATO commanders to reaffirm US support for the NATO alliance. In November and December 1973, he traveled on an official mission to Australia, Indonesia, and Singapore.[30]

During those years, Reagan made few, if any, specific comments on missile defense or the ABM negotiations and treaty. Except while travelling on Nixon's behalf, he concentrated on issues facing California. He was, however, fully briefed on nuclear weapons research. As governor of California, he was officially president of the board of regents of the University of California, and the university ran, under contract with the federal government, the two US nuclear-weapons research and development laboratories: Lawrence Livermore National Laboratory (LLNL) and the Los Alamos National Laboratory in New Mexico. By virtue of being governor of California, Reagan was thus the senior civilian supervisor, outside the federal government, of the nation's two nuclear weapons laboratories.

Edward Teller, co-founder of LLNL, recounts calling on Reagan soon after Reagan took office as governor, and Reagan's resulting visit to the lab on November 22, 1967. Reagan got a tour of the lab and a two-hour briefing on the work underway on antiballistic missiles, those designed to destroy incoming rockets as they re-enter the atmosphere and approach their targets.[31]

In spite of Nixon's considerable accomplishments, he was forced to resign over the Watergate affair (the cover-up of the break-in at the Democratic National Committee during the 1972 campaign) about five months before the end of Reagan's second term as California governor. Reagan continued to support Nixon during the Watergate affair. When William F. Buckley wired Reagan (and others) on November 6, 1973, to ask "whether *National Review* should counsel the president to resign," Reagan instructed his staff to reply with a two-word telegram: "HELL NO."[32]

Nixon's influence over Congress declined substantially during the Watergate affair, and as it did so, the US nuclear arsenal declined. It continued to do so under Presidents Ford and Carter.

Gerald R. Ford: The Second Decline: 1974–77

Gerald Ford became president when Richard Nixon resigned on August 9, 1974. The Soviets were at that point adding to their nuclear arsenal at a rate of two thousand warheads a year. By contrast, the US arsenal actually declined by about 2,500 warheads while Ford was in office.[33] In terms of numbers, ICBMs stayed the same, Submarine-Launched Ballistic Missiles increased a bit, and warheads carried on bombers declined.

Ford's statements on a US nuclear deterrent were minimal, stating only that it was important to maintain such a deterrent. He was the first president since Eisenhower not to openly warn potential aggressors that a nuclear attack—or an attack on Western Europe with conventional forces—would bring destruction to the attacker.

Ford selected Nelson Rockefeller as his vice president, a job Reagan may well have wanted. The Republican Party was in the doldrums, and Ford's pardon of Nixon was not popular. Just a few months after Ford became president, Reagan's second term as governor ended. Within a few weeks he began his daily radio program commentary, speaking to perhaps twenty million people a week on domestic and foreign issues. He also began a syndicated newspaper column and was a popular speaker around the country.

Ford made an effort to bring Reagan into his administration as a member of the cabinet or even as ambassador to Great Britain, but Reagan would have none of it—nor did he bite at the possibility of chairman of the Republican National Committee. He was interested in the presidency.

Reagan ran for the nomination of the Republican party in 1976, losing narrowly to Ford at the convention. Ford called Reagan to the podium the last night of the convention, and Reagan spoke extemporaneously: "We live in a world in which the great powers have poised and aimed at each other horrible missiles of destruction that can, in a matter of minutes, arrive in each others' country and destroy virtually the civilized world we live in."[34]

Within days of losing the nomination to Ford, Reagan returned to his daily radio commentary, his syndicated newspaper column, and speaking engagements. His first radio commentary after the August 1976 convention aired September 1, 1976.

Ford was defeated in the presidential election of 1976 by Jimmy Carter, and left him with 25,914 warheads to the 22,165 the Soviets now held.[35] Things were getting close.

The Carter Crossover: 1977–81

By the time President Jimmy Carter concluded that the Soviets were increasing their conventional forces "beyond any legitimate requirement for defense," the Soviets were also surpassing the United States in nuclear warheads. At the end of 1978, the Soviets had 26,169, the United States, 24,418.

The number of warheads isn't, of course, everything. Some of them are battlefield nuclear weapons—still immensely powerful—rather than strategic weapons. Some are taken out of service and replaced by more modern and capable weapons—more reliable, more accurate, perhaps with multiple warheads on a single delivery vehicle, greatly

Reagan at a 1965 book signing
for his first autobiography,
"Where's the Rest of Me?"
Collection of Martin Anderson.

Reagan's first campaign team the morning he announced for the presidency,
November 20, 1975. Clockwise from Reagan's left, John Sears, Nancy
Reynolds, Jeff Bell, Paul Laxalt, Peter Hannaford, Martin Anderson, Lyn
Nofziger, Michael Deaver, Richard Wirthlin, Nancy Reagan, Ronald Reagan.
Courtesy Reagan Presidential Foundation.

Reagan and Martin Anderson on the campaign trail in late 1975.
Courtesy Reagan Presidential Foundation. Photo by Michael Evans

Reagan with Ford at the August 1976 Republican National Convention.
Courtesy Reagan Presidential Foundation.

Ronald and Nancy Reagan, Martin Anderson, and Jim Lake on the November 1979 announcement trip.
Photo © Roger E. Sandler.

President Reagan on a fall 1979 flight working on one of his many speeches.
Photo by Martin Anderson.

Reagan and Martin Anderson, meeting in the Oval Office, October 1981.
Courtesy Ronald Reagan Presidential Library.

President Reagan
working at his desk
in the Oval Office,
May 1982.
*Courtesy Ronald Reagan
Presidential Library*

Reagan meeting with Pope
John Paul II in Miami,
September 1982.
*Courtesy Ronald Reagan
Presidential Library*

President Reagan and
House Speaker Tip
O'Neill discussing the
budget in the Oval Office,
January 31, 1983.
*Courtesy Ronald Reagan
Presidential Library*

President Reagan's first meeting with General Secretary Mikhail Gorbachev at Fleur D'Eau during the Geneva Summit, Switzerland, November 1985.
Ronald Reagan Presidential Library

President Reagan and Soviet leader Mikhail Gorbachev shaking hands after signing the INF Treaty in the East Room of the White House, December 8, 1987.
Courtesy Ronald Reagan Presidential Library

President Reagan speaking at Moscow State University, May 1, 1988.
Courtesy Ronald Reagan Presidential Library

Vice President George H. W. Bush, President Reagan, and General Secretary Gorbachev on Governor's Island, New York, December 1988.
Courtesy Ronald Reagan Presidential Library

President Reagan saluting as he boards the helicopter at the U.S. Capitol, Washington, D.C., on his last day as president.
Courtesy Ronald Reagan Presidential Library

President Reagan having a luncheon meeting with the Joint Chiefs of Staff—John Vessey, Edward Meyer, Robert Barrow, James Watkins, and Charles Gabriel—along with Casper Weinberger and Robert McFarlane on February 11, 1983. In his diary Reagan wrote: "out of it came a super idea. What if we tell the world we want to protect our people. . . . that we're going to embark on a program of research to come up with a defensive weapons that could make nuclear weapons obsolete?"
Courtesy Ronald Reagan Presidential Library

July 26, 1988, National Security Council meeting. Edward Teller and Lowell Wood brief President Reagan on research on brilliant pebbles, an approach to missile defense. Martin Anderson was instrumental in arranging the meeting.
Courtesy Ronald Reagan Presidential Library

President Reagan, Annelise Anderson, and Martin Anderson in the White House Roosevelt Room, February 25, 1982.
Courtesy Ronald Reagan Presidential Library.

Portrait of President Reagan by John de la Vega being presented to Martin Anderson, February 1982.
Courtesy Ronald Reagan Presidential Library.

reducing cost. Negotiators on nuclear treaties consider not only what's in place but what's on order and in the pipeline. What's proposed for development may or may not work as the designers and funders hope it will. The other side has to take this into account, make a judgment.

Intermediate-range nuclear forces, like the ones the Soviets began targeting on Western Europe in 1977, were considered non-strategic weapons—ones that could not threaten the continent on the other side of the world. They could not reach the United States from their bases in the Soviet Union (although they were mobile, and could get a little closer if they tried), but they could jettison a couple of warheads (they carried three each) and let the rocket carry only one warhead. Once they did so, they were, in fact—as the Soviets took pains to demonstrate—strategic: they could strike not only Western Europe from their locations in the Western Soviet Union, but shoot a rocket and a warhead over the North Pole to land (quite precisely, as programmed) somewhere in Canada or the United States.

Nevertheless, the Soviets strove consistently to catch up with the United States in both technical capabilities and firepower. US advances were followed in a few years, at most, by Soviet acquisition of the same capabilities.

On May 31, 1978, Carter called for a buildup of US conventional forces in Europe, but also reminded his audience that the North Atlantic Treaty Organization (NATO) had long relied on US strategic forces to deter a Warsaw Pact—especially Soviet—attack on Western Europe. "This coupling of American strategic forces to Europe is critical," he continued, "for it means that an attack on Europe would have the full consequences of an attack on the United States." In other words, the United States would retaliate. "Let there be no misunderstanding," Carter said. "The United States is prepared to use all the forces necessary for the defense of the NATO area."[36]

The year 1978 was the crossover point: the Soviets had more nuclear warheads than the United States. By the end of 1980, the United States had 24,104 nuclear warheads in its arsenal. The Soviets had 30,665, 25 percent more than the United States.[37]

Until he announced for president in November 1979, Reagan continued to deliver his syndicated radio commentary five days a week. The commentaries covered virtually every significant issue of public concern. Two-thirds of the commentaries were on domestic issues, especially the economy, Federal spending, and overregulation. One-third were on foreign policy and national defense.

A major focus of Reagan's commentaries on national defense was the second strategic arms limitation treaty (SALT II) on nuclear weapons being negotiated with the Soviet Union. Reagan wrote and delivered nineteen commentaries on SALT II and many others on national defense.

He questioned both SALT I and SALT II. "What are the facts concerning the Soviet Union?" he wrote in June 1978. "Are they what we thought they were in 1972? Do the Russians subscribe to our belief in 'mutual assured destruction' as a deterrent to war? Apparently we think so but just as apparently the Russians do not. We say, 'thermonuclear war is unthinkable by either side.' The Russians have told their own people that while it would be a calamity it is not unthinkable; that it very well might happen & if it does the Soviet U. will survive and be victorious."

Reagan was obviously not convinced that the US nuclear arsenal was adequate to deter the Soviets. He commented on one scenario developed by US experts in which Russians are evacuated from urban areas: "In the nuclear exchange that follows they lose 5% of their population—we lose 50% of ours."[38]

Reagan was clearly conversant with both the Soviet and US arsenals. He opposed SALT II on the grounds that it would actually lead to an increase in nuclear weapons to the disadvantage of the United States, which he thought was making too many concessions in the negotiations. He was also concerned that it lacked verification provisions and that it failed to cover a significant Soviet nuclear delivery system, the Backfire bomber. Reagan was no novice when it came to nuclear issues.

The SALT II treaty was signed by Carter and Soviet leader Leonid Brezhnev on June 18, 1979, but ratification by the US Senate was delayed indefinitely when the Soviets invaded Afghanistan in December 1979.

During 1979 and 1980, Reagan was campaigning for the presidency. Talking to Martin Anderson on the airplane after his July 31, 1979, tour of NORAD (the North American Aerospace Defense Command), Reagan said:

> We have spent all that money and have all that equipment, and there is nothing we can do to prevent a nuclear missile from hitting us . . . The only option a president would have would be to press the button or do nothing.
>
> They're both bad.
>
> We should have some way of defending ourselves against nuclear missiles.[39]

It was an early—and private—conversation about the threat of nuclear war. Reagan was concerned that the declining strength of the US nuclear deterrent could tempt the Soviets. The concern was expressed in a speech he gave March 17, 1980, when it was already apparent that he would be the Republican Party's nominee for president in 1980: "To prevent the ultimate catastrophe of a massive nuclear attack, we urgently need a program to preserve and restore our strategic deterrent."[40]

On June 18, 1980, Reagan told *The Washington Post* that a US arms buildup would be good for the United States because it would bring the Soviet Union to the bargaining table.[41]

Reagan defeated Carter with 50.7 percent of the popular vote to Carter's 41.0 percent. He got 489 electoral votes to Carter's 49.

Ronald Reagan and the Soviet Reversal: 1981–89

Reagan's singular accomplishment was persuading the Soviet Union that a nuclear war could not be won and must never be fought. He finally convinced Mikhail Gorbachev that an arms race was a race the

Soviets could not win, and a nuclear attack would be a disaster for the Soviet Union as well as the United States and Europe.

The Soviets had begun building nuclear weapons in 1949 and kept on doing so, with ever more powerful ways to deliver them. When Reagan took office, the Soviet nuclear arsenal was 25 percent larger than that of the United States, and the Soviets were continuing to build nuclear weapons. The Soviets added to their nuclear weapons through 1985.

The chart in this chapter shows the change Reagan wrought: the Soviets reversed their buildup after 1985. Their arsenal began to decline even before arms control agreements on intermediate-range missiles and strategic missiles were signed. Never before had the Soviets actually decreased the number of weapons in their arsenal.

Leonid Brezhnev was the general secretary of the Communist Party of the Soviet Union in 1981, when Reagan became president of the United States. Brezhnev added some two thousand warheads a year. So did his successor, Yuri Andropov, and Andropov's successor, Konstantin Chernenko.

TABLE 4   Nuclear Warheads, 1980–1988

Year	US	USSR
1980	24,104	30,062
1981	23,208	32,164
1982	22,886	33,486
1983	23,305	35,130
1984	23,495	36,825
1985	23,368	38,582
1986	23,317	35,159
1987	23,575	30,407
1988	23,205	28,288

Source: Hans M. Kristensen and Robert S. Norris, "Global Nuclear Weapons Inventories, 1945–2013," *Bulletin of the Atomic Scientists* 2013 69:75. Accessible at http://bos.sagepub.com/content/69/5/75. The article is the source data in the chart.

The buildup continued when Mikhail Gorbachev became general secretary in early 1985. By the end of that year, the Soviets had 38,582 nuclear warheads—almost two-thirds *more* than the United States, which had 23,317.[42]

Reagan did not increase the numbers in the US arsenal; the warhead count actually went down, from 24,104 in 1980, just before he took office, to 23,205 when he left.[43] But Reagan made important improvements.

Table 4 shows the number of US and Soviet nuclear warheads during the Reagan presidency.

The table demonstrates the constancy of the US arsenal and the buildup and then decline of its Soviet counterpart. The chart shows the same information, as well as the continued decline of Soviet and US arsenals after Reagan left office. The following chapters explain how he accomplished this historic change.

CHAPTER FIVE

Reagan's Decisions

We're the only country that ever dropped one of those. And that was
in World War II against Japan. But we were the only country that had
it. And you have to ask yourself, would we have dropped it if we had
known they had one they could have dropped on us? And I think we all
know the answer to that.   —*Ronald Reagan, February 25, 1983*

By the time Reagan took office, the Soviet Union had 30,062 nuclear
warheads; the United States had 24,104.[1] And the situation was actually worse from the American standpoint than the warhead count
suggested, because the Soviet weapons could do more damage than
their American counterparts.

Lowell Wood, physicist and weapons expert, writes of the opening years of Reagan's presidency: "When all components of strategic
nuclear weaponry were aggregated, the Soviet Union had at least
three times more 'deliverable megatonnage'—the explosive yield of
weapons capable of being dispatched to designated targets on the
other side of the planet, given no interference by any defensive countermeasures—than did the United States."[2, 3]

Technology, as Wood recounts, had also made the world more
dangerous. The deliverable megatonnage was MIRVed—divided into
multiple independently targetable reentry vehicles atop each rocket—
and targeting had become more precise. The MIRVed megatonnage
could thus do much more damage—specifically, to the target country's ability to retaliate—than the old-style, single warheads.

The first year of the Reagan administration—sometimes the entire
first term—is viewed by many as focused on the economy. Reagan's

economic program went into effect October 1, 1981. The two major bills, one on the budget and spending, and the other on taxes, were passed by Congress in the summer of 1981 and signed August 13, 1981, even as the recession, which began in July of that year, was beginning to take its toll.

Reagan's state of mind early in his administration comes through in his toast to Prime Minister Margaret Thatcher, his first head-of-state visitor, on February 24, 1981, at a dinner she gave at the British embassy in Washington, DC. Reagan of course honored Winston Churchill. But he also predicted that the economic difficulties of the United States and Great Britain would be overcome before long, and so, perhaps, would Communist totalitarianism:

> The gift of humor can make a people see what they might ordinarily overlook, and it supplements that other gift of great leaders—vision. When he addressed Parliament in the darkest moments after Dunkirk, Churchill dared to promise the British their finest hour and even reminded them that they would someday enjoy "the bright, sunlit uplands" from which the struggle against Hitler would be seen as only a bad memory.
>
> Well, Madam Prime Minister, you and I have heard our share of somber assessments and dire predictions in recent months. I do not refer here to the painful business of ending our economic difficulties. We know that with regard to the economies of both our countries we will be *home safe and soon enough*. I do refer, however, to those adversaries who preach the supremacy of the state.
>
> We've all heard the slogans, the end of the class struggle, the vanguard of the proletariat, the wave of the future, the inevitable triumph of socialism. Indeed, if there's anything the Marxist-Leninists might not be forgiven for, it is their willingness to bog the world down in tiresome clichés, clichés that rapidly are being recognized for what they are, a gaggle of bogus prophecies and petty superstitions. Prime Minister, everywhere one looks these days the cult of the state is dying, and I wonder if you and I and other leaders of the West should not

now be looking toward bright, sunlit uplands and begin planning for a world where our adversaries are remembered only for their role in a sad and rather bizarre chapter in human history.[4]

Although the public rhetoric focused on the economy, when we see what Reagan was actually doing and saying, it turns out that he set in motion in late 1981 the major components of his policies toward the Soviet Union, arms control, and the avoidance of nuclear war.

October, November, and December of 1981 were, behind the scenes in meetings classified secret and top secret, intensely focused on strategy—the military buildup and the strategy for dealing with the Soviets and the threat of nuclear war.

The economy was the main issue for reporters at Reagan's news conference of October 1, 1981. Nevertheless, the issue of nuclear war came up. "Mr. President," a reporter asked, "there's been talk about limited nuclear war. Do you believe that either the Soviet Union or the United States could win a nuclear war? Is there a winnable nuclear war?"

Reagan voiced his concern, as he had during the 1980 campaign, that US deterrent capabilities were tempting the Soviets to consider a first strike: "It's very difficult for me to believe that there's a winnable nuclear war, but where our great risk falls is that the Soviet Union has made it very plain that among themselves, they believe it is winnable. And believing that makes them constitute a threat, which is one of the reasons why I'm dedicated to getting them at a table not for arms limitation talks, but for arms reductions talks."[5]

The next day, Reagan announced to reporters his strategic weapons program. He planned to build one hundred B-1 bombers even as the "Stealth" aircraft was being developed, improve the sea-based Trident nuclear missiles with the D-5 warhead, and proceed with one hundred MX intercontinental ballistic missiles.

In deciding to build the B-1 bombers, Reagan overrode his secretary of defense, Caspar Weinberger. They had talked about it on June 30, 1981, when Reagan wrote in his diary: "This afternoon met with Cap. W. on the B-1. He leans toward going for the 'Stealth,' which would leave a several-year gap with only the aging B-52's. I tend to favor filling the gap with B-1's while we develop the 'Stealth.'"[6]

On October 16, 1981, at a luncheon with out-of-town editors, Reagan answered a question about the MX missile system. He explained his strategy of deterrence and building enough US strength to bring the Soviets to the bargaining table to reduce strategic weapons:

> The only real defense so far that either side has with regard to intercontinental ballistic missiles is the threat that we both represent. In other words, if we balance them enough that they know that our retaliation could be more than they want to afford, then they'll restrain from a first strike. And I suppose the same thing holds with us, although we've never taken a position that we'd ever make a first strike.
>
> In the meantime, we really mean that we're going to go forward with them and try to persuade them into a program of not limitation, but a program of actual reduction of these strategic weapons.[7]

Less than a month later, on November 15, 1981, Reagan returned from San Antonio to Washington on one of the four National Emergency Airborne Command Post (NEACP, pronounced "kneecap") planes, aircraft outfitted for command and communications to be used in the event of a nuclear attack. One of these aircraft was always close to the president. "Came home in the 747 Doomsday plane," he wrote in his diary. "Was briefed on its capabilities. It's like being in a submarine—no windows."[8]

On November 18, 1981, Reagan gave a major address on arms control at Washington's National Press Club, expressing his objectives of reduction in strategic and conventional weapons, and specifically presenting what became known as his zero-zero proposal for intermediate-range nuclear weapons in Europe. "The United States," he said, "is prepared to cancel its deployment of Pershing II and ground-launched cruise missiles if the Soviets will dismantle their SS-20, SS-4, and SS-5 missiles."[9]

On December 3, 1981, Reagan received the classified information that 150 million residents would be killed in an all-out nuclear attack on the United States. On December 14, he met with the Vatican's study team reporting on the devastating effects of a nuclear war.

The next day, Reagan met with Cardinal Casaroli, the Vatican secretary of state. They talked about the declaration of martial law in Poland only two days earlier. Casaroli expressed the view that "the time was not yet ripe" for major change in Eastern Europe. The president and the cardinal also talked about nuclear war. Reagan noted that there was "no miracle weapon available with which to deal with the Soviets," but added that the Soviets could be threatened by the US ability to outbuild them. "The only way to deter nuclear war is to arm as strongly as the potential opponent," Reagan said.

Reagan was clearly letting Casaroli—and the Pope—know that détente was over. But the horrors of nuclear war remained on Reagan's mind, and he mentioned his meeting of the day before: "I was struck by the Papal report's conclusion that in the event of nuclear war there would be no way to care for the huge number of wounded."[10]

Reagan's Soviet policy was set during the latter months of 1981. His primary strategy was a military buildup that would make any nuclear offensive by the Soviets so damaging to the Soviets that they would not be tempted to undertake it; and to therefore encourage weapons reductions—verifiable ones—on both sides.

Reagan talked about his policy of deterrence in a classified April 21, 1982, meeting of the National Security Council: "You look at Russian history. Protecting the homeland has always been of paramount importance. If they know that we might respond to them by hitting them anywhere in the world, that's a strong deterrent."[11]

He concluded: "We will do whatever is necessary to meet our objectives. A vigorous defense buildup will also be a great help at arms control talks. The Soviets do not believe that they can keep up with us."[12]

Meanwhile, Reagan wanted to make sure the Soviets had no doubts about what would happen to them if they struck first. Speaking to the West German parliament—the *Bundestag*—in Bonn, on June 9, 1982, about the threat of retaliation as a deterrent, he said: "Deterrence has kept the peace, and we must continue to take the steps necessary to make deterrence credible. . . . Our adversaries would be foolishly mistaken should they gamble that Americans would abandon their Alliance responsibilities, no matter how severe the test."[13] Besides stating a continuing and crucial US commitment, Reagan was preparing European leaders for the introduction of Pershing II and cruise missiles as a counterthreat to the Soviet missiles targeted on Western European cities.

On February 25, 1983, Reagan did a question-and-answer session with high school students visiting the White House. Reagan's meetings with students are among his most spontaneous and unscripted remarks; unlike formal press conferences, he did not work with staff on potential questions and answers. On this White House occasion, a student from Lake Oswego High School in Oregon said that his generation was very concerned with nuclear war: "To tell you the truth, we're sort of scared." Reagan got right into it:

> I know the fear that everyone has. . . . The only defense you have is being able to say, if one of you does it the other one's going to do it, too. And there is no winner.

On intermediate-range weapons in Europe, Reagan said, "they [the Soviets] have a monopoly. They are the only ones with the threat." The zero option was on the table: US Pershings and cruise missiles would deploy if the Soviets didn't remove their weapons. And Reagan noted that "I think they came to the table and are willing to talk because they don't want us to put in that deterrent. . . . But I would say here . . . I believe that for 37 years we've proven that that deterrent idea does work. And I'm still confident of that."

He continued: "Let me point out, we're the only country that ever dropped one of those [nuclear bombs]. And that was in the World War II against Japan. But we were the only country that had it. And you have to ask yourself, would we have dropped it if we had known they had one they could have dropped on us? And I think we all know the answer to that. So, we're not completely helpless."[14]

In fact, Reagan was getting ready to announce his Strategic Defense Initiative (SDI), a research effort to develop a defense against nuclear missiles. He told the students that nuclear weapons were "the first weapon ever invented that has never, at the same time, led to a defensive weapon against it."[15] Reagan was well on his way to trying to change that. The SDI announcement was only a month away, and Reagan had already met twice with the Joint Chiefs of Staff on this matter—on December 22, 1982, and again on February 11, 1983.

From the beginning, he hated the policy of "mutual assured destruction," even as he relied on it. His search for an alternative led to the SDI, which was announced on March 23, 1983. Reagan was clear at the outset that it would take perhaps decades for the SDI to become a reality, if it was possible at all. But he regarded the system as a way to make nuclear weapons obsolete and to protect against the possibility of an attack by a rogue state or one intentionally violating its international commitments.

Making nuclear weapons obsolete was Reagan's ultimate goal. He spoke often of it as his dream. He also made clear from the outset that his intent was to share the technology with the world. On March 29, 1983, only six days after the announcement of the research program, he told reporters in the Oval Office:

I am determined to continue doing everything I can to persuade them [the Soviets] that legitimate arms reduction is the only path to follow. To look down to an endless future with both of us sitting here with these horrible missiles aimed at each other, and the only thing preventing a holocaust is no one pulling the trigger. This is unthinkable. . . .

If a defensive weapon could be found and developed that would reduce the utility of these, or maybe even make them obsolete, then whenever the time came, a President of the United States would be able to say, 'Now, we have both the deterrent, the missile—as we've had in the past—but now this other thing that has altered this.' And he could follow any one of a number of courses. He could offer to give that same defensive weapon to them, to prove to them that there was no longer any need for keeping these missiles.

Or with that defense, he could then say to them, 'I am willing to do away with all my missiles. You do away with all of yours.'[16]

The more immediate goal of arms control negotiations was the reduction of nuclear arsenals on both sides.

In the November 30, 1983, NSC meeting on SDI, Reagan expressed his hopes and his fears about nuclear weapons. He was clearly convinced that if the Soviets succeeded in developing a defense against nuclear missiles, they would threaten the world with their offensive nuclear arsenal; by contrast, if the United States had defense as well as offense, it would be an opportunity to end the threat of nuclear destruction.

"I agree with Secretary Shultz," Reagan said in the meeting, "that we are charting a new program. To take an optimistic view, if the US is first to have both offense and defense, we could put the nuclear genie back into the bottle—by volunteering to eliminate offensive weapons. . . .

"We are not alone, and the Soviets really make this decision for us. How are we to face the day when they have both offensive weapons and an effective defense?"[17]

When Pershing II and cruise missiles arrived in Western Europe to counter the threat of similar Soviet weapons targeted on Western European cities, the Soviets walked out of the arms control talks. The date was December 8, 1983. Reagan was ready with a quotation from Eisenhower's 1953 "Atoms for Peace" speech. He had written it out by hand on a 3 × 5 card he kept as part of a collection in his desk. As he stopped to answer reporters' questions that day, he said:

It was just 30 years ago today, on December 8th, 1953, that President Dwight Eisenhower made a speech on this very subject of nuclear weapons. And in that speech, he said, "To the making of these fateful decisions, the United States pledges before you . . . its determination to help solve the fearful atomic dilemma—to devote its entire heart and mind to find the way by which the miraculous inventiveness of man shall not be dedicated to his death, but consecrated to his life."

And this administration endorses this view completely, and this is what we are dedicated to.[18]

In his January 16, 1984, speech, Reagan again spoke about eliminating nuclear weapons. It was his strongest statement yet on the subject, but it was still a dream:

Living in the nuclear age makes it imperative that we do talk. In our approach to negotiations, reducing the risk of war, and especially nuclear war, is priority number one. A nuclear conflict could well be mankind's last. . . .

Indeed, I support a zero option for all nuclear arms.

As I've said before, my dream is to see the day when nuclear weapons will be banished from the face of the Earth. . . . [19]

As Reagan's military buildup proceeded, he grew more confident in the effectiveness of the US deterrent. As mentioned above, one hundred B-1 bombers were on order, the stealth plane was under development, MX missiles with increased targeting capabilities were being built, and submarines were scheduled to be equipped with more powerful and accurate Trident missiles.

In a February 2, 1984, interview with Robert L. Bartley and Robert R. Hunt of *The Wall Street Journal*, Reagan expressed his confidence in US deterrent capabilities:

. . . the only way that we were going to convince them that common sense called for a reduction of arms was to build our own defenses to where we had a deterrent capacity, but to make it evident that we were going to maintain a deterrent policy. They would then have to look and say, how much would they have to build to try and get a sufficient advantage over us, and I don't think they can. And I think that they know that. They know the industrial might of this nation.[20]

On September 26, 1984, Reagan spoke briefly at Bowling Green State University in Ohio:

> With our neighbors and allies, we've made ourselves open to dialogue and eager to be of assistance.... To our adversaries too, we must remain open. But there, an additional element is called for—firmness—so that our adversaries neither miscalculate our responses nor misjudge our resolve.... During the past few years we've once again shown our firmness and steadiness....
>
> The world is a dangerous place. We try to be a good neighbor, but we must be strong enough and confident enough to be patient when provoked. But we must be equally clear that past a certain point, our adversaries push us at their peril. Uncle Sam is a friendly old man, but he has a spine of steel....
>
> We should remember the central lesson of World War II. Our allies tried very hard for peace, to the point of outright appeasement. If only they'd shown Germany early on that they would pay any price and bear any burden to ensure the survival of their liberties, then Britain might not have known the blitz and Dresden might not have known the flames....
>
> From our earliest years, our Presidents have stressed the crucial role of strength in promoting stability. George Washington said, "There is nothing so likely to produce peace as to be well-prepared to meet a foe." He said we should remember that "timely disbursements to prepare for danger frequently prevent much greater disbursements to repel it."
>
> Much closer to our own times, John Kennedy said: "The primary purpose of our arms is peace, not war. Our preparation against danger is our hope of safety."
>
> Well, we live in the age of nuclear arms, and the question of what to do about nuclear weapons is deeply frustrating for Americans. We're a nation of problem solvers. And here we are faced with a problem that, so far, has resisted our best efforts.
>
> Some propose unilateral disarmament: We disarm in the hope the other side will follow. Well, there are great saints and great sinners

among us. Historically, unilateral disarmament has never worked; it has only encouraged aggressors.

It's frustrating, but here is the truth of the nuclear age: there are no cheap solutions, no easy answers. The only path to progress on this is the open door, the honest proposal, and such a path takes patience. But patience isn't inappropriate. Each day the world turns completely. Each day the world is reborn. Possibilities that yesterday didn't exist emerge and startle us.[21]

Reagan was crystal clear in his October 21, 1984, presidential campaign debate with Vice President Walter F. Mondale in Kansas City, Missouri:

The Soviet Union has been engaged in the biggest military buildup in the history of man at the same time that we tried the policy of unilateral disarmament, of weakness, if you will. And now we are putting up a defense of our own. And I've made it very plain to them, we seek no superiority. We simply are going to provide a deterrent so that it will be too costly for them if they are nursing any ideas of aggression against us.[22]

In the same debate, Reagan reiterated his willingness to share strategic defensive systems and his ultimate goal—his dream—of eliminating nuclear weapons:

Why not? . . . I think that would be the greatest use of a defensive weapon. . . . Here's what we can do. Now, if you're willing to join us in getting rid of all the nuclear weapons in the world, then we'll give you this one, so that we could both know that no one can cheat . . . I think the world will be better off. . . .

I have said that it seems to me that this could be a logical step in what is my ultimate goal, my ultimate dream, and that is the elimination of nuclear weapons in the world."[23]

In a secret December 5, 1984, meeting of the National Security Planning Group, Reagan said: "It is important to link research on SDI to making nuclear weapons obsolete . . . SDI is a non-nuclear defensive system. I still wonder whether or not we could give them the technology. SDI gives us a great deal of leverage on the Soviet Union."[24]

Quoting further from the minutes of that meeting:

> We and the Soviet Union may be coming together more than many people realized. We have never believed that we would find ourselves at war with Russia except to defend ourselves against attack. . . . Everything they have says that they are looking at a first strike because it is they, not we, who have built up both offensive and defensive systems. We could build on the Soviet preoccupation with protecting the homeland by making clear that we have no intention of starting a nuclear war. . . . Both sides have indicated that they would like to get rid of nuclear weapons entirely, but they are afraid of SDI.[25]

In an interview in the Oval Office with Bernard Weinraub and Gerald Boyd of the *New York Times* on February 11, 1985—after Reagan had won re-election and the Soviets had agreed to come back to the bargaining table—the questioners were direct: "Are we going into negotiations [on arms control] in a position of inferiority?"

Reagan replied by readily agreeing that the Soviets had superior military strength. But he said he was confident that, as the parties returned to the bargaining table, the United States was in a stronger bargaining position than it had been:

> We have fewer warheads than we had in 1967. But I think, in one way, we're going in in a stronger sense . . . with the refurbishing of our military defenses that we've been undergoing for these four years, we're going to the table, and they have the knowledge that not only are we stronger than we were, even though we have not caught up with them as yet, but they have the awareness that we're determined not to allow them to have a superiority over us to the extent that our forces wouldn't be a deterrent. . . .
>
> We are not cancelling weapons systems without getting anything in return . . . they can look down the road and see that there's a point

at which they won't have any margin of superiority. . . . And they don't have enough of a margin today to tempt them into a first strike.[26]

To Lou Cannon, Dave Hoffman, and Len Downie of *The Washington Post*, on April 1, 1985, Reagan commented on the progress the United States had made in deterrence, but reiterated his conviction that Soviet military strength exceeded that of the United States:

> I've heard some spokesmen, and some who should know better, in and out of government . . . voicing their opinions that somehow we're on a parity with the Soviet Union. This is the most ridiculous thing I've ever heard. The Soviet Union virtually outnumbers us in any type of weapon you want to name, has consistently modernized their land-based nuclear missiles. . . . They are about 3 to 1 in megatonnage, nuclear megatonnage, over us. They outnumber us in conventional weapons in almost every category. Their navy has several hundred more ships than we have.
>
> We've been making progress. We think that we've achieved, I think, a deterrent to the effect that they'd have to think twice about taking us on. But we haven't caught up with them or surpassed them in any sense.[27]

Chatting with members of the American Legion Auxiliary's Girls Nation on July 18, 1986, in the Rose Garden, Reagan recalled, as he often did, the four wars in his lifetime: "Not one of them started because this country was too strong. Mainly, they started because others thought we wouldn't defend our rights or our freedom." He went on to restate a major theme of his second term, his hopes for strategic defense:

> We don't intend to make the same mistake. . . . Today if a foreign country were to launch a nuclear attack on America, a President would be forced to respond in kind. But the research program we've begun could produce the means to destroy the incoming nuclear weapons before they reached our country and without launching a counterattack of our

own, thereby saving millions of lives in our own nation and in other nations.[28]

In remarks to students gathered at Fort McHenry in Baltimore, on October 15, 1986, Reagan explained the necessity of being prepared and his hopes for SDI:

> Unfortunately, today most Americans don't realize that our country has no defense at all against the deadliest weapons of our day: nuclear-tipped missiles, intercontinental ballistic missiles. Somebody pushes a button, and a half hour later our world is blowing up... And by the time you high school students are finished with your education, a new technology may be available that will make this a far safer world than the one we're living in today, one in which the danger of nuclear war will not cast a shadow over your lives as it has over ours.[29]

Reagan's commitment to strategic defense continued throughout his administration. Even after the signing of the Intermediate-Range Nuclear Forces Treaty in 1987 and the summit meeting in Moscow in 1988, on August 3, 1989, he vetoed the defense authorization act for 1989 because it limited research programs on SDI he considered essential.

To summarize, Reagan began his administration with concern about the US nuclear deterrent. As the nation's military upgrades proceeded, he grew more confident about both the deterrent effect of the US arsenal and its effect in persuading the Soviets to negotiate reductions.

CHAPTER SIX

Negotiating to End the Cold War

Once it became clear—or at least highly likely—that Ronald Reagan would be re-elected president of the United States in 1984, the Soviets decided they'd better deal with him.

Their first move was to indicate that they'd accept an invitation from President Reagan for their foreign minister, Andrei Gromyko, to meet with Reagan in September, when the United Nations opened its 1984 session. The Soviet foreign minister had met with the US president every year until the Soviets invaded Afghanistan in December 1979, when the invitations were withdrawn. Reagan reinstated the offer, Gromyko accepted, and they met on September 28, 1984.

Reagan wrote his own talking points for the meeting, and during it, he told Gromyko:

> We both know that other countries have turned to nuclear weapons and more are quietly working to achieve that goal. The danger of such proliferation is the possibility of accidental war brought on by neither of us but triggering a conflict that could ultimately involve us both. But what if we who have the power to destroy the world should join in saving it? If we can reach agreement on reducing and ultimately eliminating these weapons, we could persuade the rest of the world to join us in doing away with all such weapons.[1,2]

Following Reagan's re-election—when he won forty-nine states, losing only Walter Mondale's home state of Minnesota, and won 58.8 percent of the popular vote—the general secretary of the Soviet Communist party, Konstantin Chernenko, wrote Reagan a letter of congratulations. Chernenko followed that with a second letter stating that the Soviets were willing to resume arms control talks and that in fact they agreed with Reagan on the goal of abolishing nuclear weapons.

Reagan's strategy was to take them at their word so that he could call them on it later. Mikhail Gorbachev, waiting in the wings for the frail Chernenko's imminent death from emphysema, repeated the goal of abolishing nuclear weapons in a speech in London, where he went in December 1984 to meet with Margaret Thatcher, Great Britain's prime minister.

Although the Soviets had voiced agreement with Reagan's ultimate goal of abolishing nuclear weapons, they didn't want the United States to proceed with its Strategic Defense Initiative. On December 21, 1984, Reagan responded to reporters asking about the objections to SDI (Strategic Defense Initiative) of both Thatcher and French President François Mitterrand:

> Well, I'll get them to understand what it is, too. Today the only defensive weapon we have is to threaten that if they kill millions of our people, we'll kill millions of theirs.
>
> I don't think there's any morality in that at all. We're trying to look for something that will make those weapons obsolete, and they can be eliminated once and for all.[3]

Talking to Thatcher, Reagan maintained his commitment to SDI and to his ultimate goal:

> We cannot and should not have to go on living under the threat of nuclear destruction. We must eliminate the threat posed by strategic nuclear weapons. My ultimate goal is to eliminate nuclear weapons. . . . We also know that in a nuclear war there would be no winners.[4]

The US-Soviet arms-control talks were set to resume on March 12, 1985. Chernenko died on March 10, succumbing to the ravages of his illness. The Politburo met the next day, with the result that Mikhail

Gorbachev finally became general secretary of the party and the leader of the Soviet Union.

On March 14, 1985, Reagan commented on the arms control negotiations: ". . . the Soviet Union is . . . back at the bargaining table on arms reductions because they recognize a hard, cold fact, and that is that the United States isn't going to unilaterally disarm in the face of their military buildup. . . ."[5]

Reagan sent a letter congratulating Gorbachev the day after his election and invited him to visit Washington. They exchanged a dozen or so letters in the following months. Reagan argued that his strategic defense initiative had only defensive, not offensive, purposes, whereas the Soviets already had the only operational Anti-Ballistic Missile system, and continued to upgrade it and pursue ABM research.

In response, Gorbachev called the US research effort an attempt to develop "attack space weapons." He proposed in one letter that the two sides agree to "a complete ban on space attack weapons, and a truly radical reduction, say by 50 percent, of their corresponding nuclear arms."[6] Both leaders expressed the view that nuclear war would be a catastrophe for both nations.

On September 20, 1985, Reagan chaired a National Security Council meeting in preparation for the Geneva Summit, to which Gorbachev had agreed in July. Reagan concluded:

> I believe SDI may very well be our most important leverage.
>
> I am prepared, once any of our SDI programs proved out, to then announce to the world that integrating these weapons in our respective arsenals would put international relations on a more stable footing.
>
> In fact, this could even lead to a complete elimination of nuclear weapons.
>
> We must be prepared to tell the world that we are ready to consult and negotiate on integrating these weapons into a new defense philosophy, and to state openly that we are ready to internationalize these systems.[7]

Reagan had been proposing substantial (and verifiable) reductions in strategic weapons since 1981. He wrote in his diary about the National Security Planning Group (NSPG) meeting of October 22, 1985 (another gathering to prepare for the Geneva summit):

> My own idea is that we undermine their propaganda plan by offering a counter proposal which stresses our acceptance of some of their figures—such as a 50% cut in weapons & a total of 6,000 warheads etc.
> Those are pretty much like what we've already proposed.[8]

In a memo Reagan wrote for himself about the upcoming summit, he noted that "another of our goals probably stated to Gorbachev in private should be that failure to come to a solid, verifiable arms reduction agreement will leave no alternative except an arms race and there is no way we will allow them to win such a race."[9]

Reagan and Gorbachev finally met in Geneva, Switzerland, on November 19–20, 1985. Reagan greeted Gorbachev warmly on the steps of the villa where most of the meetings were to take place. He opened the first of their two private meetings (private except for note takers and translators) by remarking that the two of them came from similar beginnings—farm communities—and now held the fate of the world in their hands as the leaders of the only two countries who could start World War III, but also the only two that could bring peace to the world.

In their second private meeting—in the boathouse in front of a fire—Reagan presented Gorbachev with written proposals on the 50 percent reduction in strategic nuclear weapons. Gorbachev quickly agreed but emphasized the dependence of the reductions on US willingness to kill SDI, which he called "space weapons."

Reagan countered that the results of research on strategic defense—which would include testing— would be shared by all. "The worst thing that I can imagine is for any one country to acquire a first-strike capability." He proposed that their negotiators draw up an agreement that the two of them would sign "not to retain a monopoly of defensive weapons."

Gorbachev wanted an agreement to stop any research or testing on what he continued to call space weapons. He wanted an official statement to that effect, along with a 50 percent reduction in "offensive arms."

Reagan argued that "we should go forward to rid the world of the threat of nuclear weapons." Gorbachev responded that the Soviet Union "would seek to counter your SDI in any possible way—including by increasing the numbers of its offensive arms . . . it is clear that strategic defense would only be useful after a first strike by the side deploying such defense."[10]

As they walked together from the boathouse, Reagan proposed a summit in the United States and then a 1987 summit in the Soviet Union. Gorbachev accepted.

It is likely on this walk, out of earshot of everyone except translators, that Reagan also advised Gorbachev that the United States would not allow the Soviet Union to win an arms race. To quote again from Martin Anderson's July 25, 1989, interview with Reagan:

> I said to him . . . We can continue to disarm or we can continue the arms race. And I'll tell you now, you can't win the arms race. There is no way. There's no way that we're going to allow you to maintain supremacy . . . over the United States of America. . . . [11]

In their joint statement after the summit, issued on November 21, 1985, Reagan and Gorbachev "agreed that a nuclear war cannot be won and must never be fought."[12] It was a sentiment Reagan had first voiced in an April 1982, five-minute radio address to the nation.

The two leaders exchanged cordial letters in the following months, but little happened until January 15, 1986, when Gorbachev announced a plan for "ridding the Earth of nuclear weapons . . . within the next 15 years, before the end of this century."[13] It included a ban on SDI development, testing, and deployment plus other arrangements that left the United States and Europe vulnerable and dependent on the good will of the Soviets to carry out its promises. Gorbachev was trying to gain the high ground and pressure Reagan into negotiating an agreement favorable to the Soviet Union.

Reagan declined to call that a publicity stunt. Instead, he expressed agreement with the ultimate goals and reiterated his commitment to the continuation of the SDI.

Gorbachev wrote on April 2, 1986, asking for a "single-purpose" meeting with Reagan on nuclear testing—not a substitute for the major meetings they'd agreed upon at Geneva. Reagan wrote back suggesting that the issue be taken up at lower levels.

And then, on April 26, 1986, came the explosion at one of the reactors at the Chernobyl nuclear power plant, with radioactive fallout damaging large areas in Ukraine, Belarus, and Russia, and reaching as far as Eastern and Western Europe as well. Gorbachev wrote Reagan—in yet another of their exchanges to get negotiations going—that "What occurred at Chernobyl served as a serious reminder of the terrible forces contained in the energy of the atom."[14]

Although Reagan wanted to persuade the Soviets that the United States did not seek a first-strike capability, he also wanted to continue with SDI research and testing, linking SDI deployment to the elimination of nuclear weapons. Since Reagan took office, the Soviets had added over six thousand warheads to their own bombers, submarines, intercontinental ballistic missiles in silos, and mobile launchers with weapons targeted on Western Europe. The US stockpile had remained virtually the same size.

Reagan sent Gorbachev more specific proposals on July 25, 1986. Then, on September 15, Gorbachev again requested a meeting, supposedly preparatory to a summit, and Reagan agreed. Of the two locations Gorbachev suggested, Reagan chose Reykjavik, Iceland, instead of London.

The minutes of Reagan's October 7, 1986, NSPG meeting have not been released. Memos sent to Reagan (e.g., by Stephen Sestanovich of the National Security Council) show that the Americans were uncertain about what Gorbachev's strategy and tactics would be in Reykjavik.[15]

However, Anatoly Chernayaev—Gorbachev's senior foreign policy aide—kept a diary and notes on meetings. Chernayaev reports Gorbachev's instructions: "[W]e must emphasize that we are proposing the liquidation of nuclear weapons, which we already discussed with the President in Geneva." Gorbachev concluded that ". . . for ourselves first and foremost keep in mind the task of knocking the Pershing II's out of Europe. It is a gun pressed to our temple."

As the discussion at the meeting continued, Gorbachev stated that "Our goal is to prevent the next round of arms race. . . . And if we do not compromise on some questions, even very important ones, we will lose the main point: we will be pulled into an arms race beyond our power, and we will lose this race, for we are presently at the limit of our capabilities."[16]

Gorbachev's ultimate goal was to prevent US weapons in space and dissuade the United States from withdrawing from the ABM treaty. "We should concentrate all our resources on the development of our own anti-SDI, [we should] give people material incentives. We must not allow the US superiority in this issue."[17] Clearly, SDI was a major Soviet concern. Gorbachev added that "Our position will be the following: if there is no agreement about directives for negotiations, there will be no Gorbachev visit to the States. This is the hook on which we can hold Reagan."[18]

The meeting in Reykjavik was announced September 30, and it took place October 11 and 12, 1986. Reagan argued for a revised ABM treaty in which each side would agree to share the results of a defensive system. In a memorable exchange, he said he would share SDI with the Soviets—and Gorbachev replied that he didn't believe Reagan. That brought this retort from the US president: "If I thought that SDI could not be shared, I would have rejected it myself."[19]

They talked about intermediate-range weapons in Europe and Asia and about strategic weapons. They agreed on 50 percent reductions in strategic weapons and even on the possibility of eventually eliminating nuclear weapons. But Gorbachev made everything conditional on confining SDI to the laboratory. Reagan refused and ended the meeting.

Although the Reykjavik summit concluded without an agreement, what Gorbachev had put on the table stayed on the table. On his return from Reykjavik, Reagan told the nation why he refused to bargain away his strategic defense initiative for Soviet promises to reduce nuclear weapons—in the future:

> Some years ago, the United States and the Soviet Union agreed to limit any defense against nuclear missile attacks to the emplacement in one location in each country of a small number of missiles capable of intercepting and shooting down incoming nuclear missiles, thus leaving our real defense—a policy called mutual assured destruction, meaning if one side launched a nuclear attack, the other side would retaliate. And this mutual threat of destruction was believed to be a deterrent against either side striking first. So here we sit, with thousands of nuclear warheads targeted on each other and capable of wiping out both our countries. The Soviets deployed the few antiballistic missiles around Moscow as the treaty permitted. Our country didn't bother deploying because the threat of nationwide annihilation made such a limited defense seem useless.
>
> And let me return again to the SDI issue. I realize some Americans may be asking tonight: why not accept Mr. Gorbachev's demand? Why not give up SDI for this agreement? Well, the answer, my friends, is simple. SDI is America's insurance policy that the Soviet Union would keep the commitments made at Reykjavik. SDI is America's security guarantee if the Soviets should—as they have done in the past—fail to comply with their solemn commitments. SDI is what brought the Soviets back to arms control talks at Geneva and Iceland. SDI is the key to a world without nuclear weapons. The Soviets understand this. They have devoted far more resources, for a lot longer time than we, to their own SDI. The world's only operational missile defense today surrounds Moscow, the capital of the Soviet Union.[20]

Several months later—on February 28, 1987—Gorbachev agreed to negotiate the elimination of intermediate-range weapons in Europe *without* the condition that the United States first abandon all but laboratory research on SDI. But progress was slow. Although Reagan had invited Gorbachev to a summit in Washington, he had not accepted, and the Soviets continued to stall in the treaty negotiations.

Finally, on October 27, Reagan wrote in his diary: "The Soviets blinked. Shevardnadze speaking for Gorbachev is arriving Thurs. for meetings on INF [the Intermediate-Range Nuclear Forces treaty] and plans for the summit."[21]

Eduard Shevardnadze, the Soviet minister of foreign affairs, did indeed arrive with a letter from Gorbachev accepting Reagan's invitation. A summit meeting was quickly agreed to and announced on October 30, and on December 7, 1987, Gorbachev arrived in the United States.

The Soviet leader enjoyed his visit. Huge and enthusiastic crowds gathered on Washington, DC's, Pennsylvania Avenue to see him drive by. He got out of his limousine spontaneously and shook some hands.

Overall, the summit proved to be a success. The INF treaty, signed in the East Room of the White House on December 8, eliminated an entire class of nuclear weapons, and it became the first treaty between the United States and the Soviet Union to actually reduce nuclear weapons rather than merely limit their future increase. Reagan had initially proposed the zero-zero option for intermediate-range weapons on November 18, 1981, more than six years earlier.[22]

CHAPTER SEVEN

The Moscow Summit and the End of the Cold War, 1988

The signing of the Intermediate-Range Nuclear Forces (INF) treaty marked a huge accomplishment for Reagan, but the biggest arms-control issue remained on the table: the 50 percent reduction of the huge US and Soviet stockpiles of intercontinental ballistic missiles (ICBMs), with their multiple warheads. Gorbachev had agreed with Reagan in principle about reducing the stockpiles. But working out the details of a strategic arms reduction treaty (START) was complicated, difficult, and sure to be lengthy. For example, in the critical area of verification, the Soviets had 1,800 sites involved with ICBMs, many more than the 150 sites with which the INF treaty dealt.

Preparing for the Moscow Summit

On February 9, 1988, Reagan chaired a classified meeting of his National Security Planning Group (NSPG) in the Situation Room. He and twenty-three key advisors and negotiators discussed the US options for arms reduction at the upcoming summit in Moscow in May. Reagan began by laying his thoughts on the table:

> If the Soviets and we have a Moscow summit, it could be the most important meeting of all. We now have a range of arms control options, but depending on how we use our time, our options will narrow. I need your honest assessments of what we can and should achieve in Moscow. . . .
>
> I know how much must be accomplished before we can conclude [an] arms agreement with the Soviets.
>
> I will not rush to an agreement for agreement's sake. . . .[1]

Reagan listened to General Colin Powell and Secretary of State George Shultz express their views for about fifteen minutes. He then drew on his extensive negotiating experience to outline the process he thought the US team should follow:

> From my past experiences as a labor negotiator, maybe we need to do this. We need to go for the gold.
>
> You need to put down what the ideal agreement would be. After you have done that, you can decide among ourselves what our bottom lines should be—what we can and what we can't give up. . . . those items on which we can't bargain. And we should set up the things that are not essential.
>
> Now, once you have that, then you can see the negotiating pattern of what you absolutely must get, what you could try for but you'd still have a good agreement if you didn't get, but the bottom line is you've got to go for the gold.
>
> There are things that we simply can't retreat on. One of them is verification. . . .[2]

Reagan introduced the idea that, partly as a result of the April 1986 explosion at the Chernobyl nuclear power plant, the Soviets were becoming more aware of how devastating an exchange of nuclear weapons would be:

> We must not ignore certain things. First of all, the situation is not the same as in INF. In this case, the Soviets want a START Treaty too. In INF we were the demanders. They had the SS-20's. We had to force them out of them. But in this case, it's very evident that they, too, want a START agreement. They feel they need START. In that context, I can't be too pessimistic. One thing of interest is that they have an innate eye to protect the homeland at all cost, and it may be that they recognized after Chernobyl that facing the nuclear force they face, they can't do this.
>
> So I think we must press.[3]

General Powell summed up what Reagan was saying: "I think we have, therefore, Mr. President, a decision that we'll go for the gold."[4]

On May 23, Reagan chaired the final NSPG meeting before the Moscow Summit, which was to begin six days later. The range and complexity of issues had made it impossible to finalize a treaty on strategic arms, but Reagan wanted work on that to continue, and he stated clearly how important he viewed his arms control policy:

> Looking to the future, even though we weren't able to have START and Defense and Space treaties ready for signature at this meeting, we mustn't stop our efforts.
>
> I want to leave as a legacy as complete and coherent an arms reduction position as I can.[5]

The Moscow Summit

This summit meeting, held May 29 through June 1, 1988, was a dramatic event.

After the two leaders held a very warm initial meeting at the Kremlin, Reagan and wife, Nancy, decided to walk along the Arbat, a Moscow shopping street where musicians, artists, and street vendors congregated. (The Secret Service objected.) They were recognized and welcomed by friendly Russians. The only hostility came from the KGB—toward the crowd; Reagan noted in his diary the organization's "brutal manhandling [of] their own people, who were in no way getting out of hand."

Reagan met with Gorbachev for a second time the next day, visited the Danilov Monastery, where he spoke to the monks about the need for freedom of worship, and then went back to the residence at the US embassy to meet with dissidents and "refusniks." Gorbachev hosted dinner at the Kremlin.

Reagan and Gorbachev met again privately the next day (May 31), and both attended the larger meeting of those involved in the summit. Gorbachev took Reagan on a walk among the crowds in Red Square.

The Russians on hand for the event were delighted. When a reporter asked Reagan about his "Evil Empire" statement, Reagan said, "I was talking about another time, another era."

In the afternoon, Reagan spoke—under a bust of Lenin—to more than one thousand students and faculty at Moscow State University about freedom and the opportunities that awaited them. He got a standing ovation. That night the Reagans gave a dinner for the Gorbachevs. The following night, the two couples attended the Bolshoi Ballet, where the orchestra played the "Star-Spangled Banner." Reagan and Nancy visited Red Square on their way back from a dinner at Gorbachev's dacha.

At their June 1 meeting, Reagan and Gorbachev exchanged signed copies of the INF treaty, which had been ratified by the US Senate only days before—on May 27. The treaty came into effect with this June 1 exchange of documents.

Meanwhile, the joint statement for the Moscow summit was modified to eliminate two words—"peaceful co-existence"—to which Reagan objected. The final, eleven-page statement, also issued on June 1, included these key paragraphs:

> Assessing the state of US-Soviet relations, the President and the General Secretary underscored the historic importance of their meetings in Geneva, Reykjavik, Washington, and Moscow in laying the foundation for a realistic approach to the problems of strengthening stability and reducing the risk of conflict.
>
> They reaffirmed their solemn conviction that a nuclear war cannot be won and must never be fought, their determination to prevent any war between the United States and Soviet Union, whether nuclear or conventional, and their disavowal of any intention to achieve military superiority.
>
> The two leaders are convinced that the expanding political dialogue they have established . . . can serve as a constructive basis for addressing not only the problems of the present, but of tomorrow and the next century. It is a process which the President and the General Secretary believe serves the best interests of the peoples of the United States and

the Soviet Union, and can contribute to a more stable, more peaceful and safer world."[6]

Sixteen men and women–eight Americans and eight Soviets–contributed to this historic statement.

For the Americans:
George P. Shultz, Secretary of State
Frank C. Carlucci, Secretary of Defense
Howard H. Baker, Presidential Chief of Staff
Colin L. Powell, National Security Adviser
Paul H. Nitze, Adviser on Arms Control Matters
Edward L. Rowny, Ambassador on Arms Control
Jack F. Matlock, Ambassador of the US to the USSR
Rozanne L. Ridgway, Assistant Secretary of State
For the Soviets (many from the Politburo):
Andrei A. Gromyko, Chairman of the USSR Supreme Soviet
Eduard A. Shevardnadze, Minister of Foreign Affairs of the USSR
Alexander N. Yakovlev, CPSU Central Committee
Dimitri T. Yazov, Minister of Defense
Anatoly F. Dobrynin, CPSU Central Committee
Anatoly S. Chernyaev, Assistant to Gorbachev
Alexander A. Bessmertnykh, Deputy Minister of Foreign Affairs
Yuri V. Dubinin, Ambassador of the USSR to the US

The extraordinary changes that led to the end of the Cold War took place over many years, beginning in 1981. But on June 1, 1988, in Moscow the two leaders put together a joint statement that, for all essential purposes, simply said that the Cold War had ended. The key line they both endorsed said they both were determined "to prevent any war between the United States and Soviet Union, whether nuclear or conventional" and to disavow "any intention to achieve military superiority."[7] No war, no nuclear weapons, no conventional weapons, and no military superiority. It does sound like the Cold War ended on that warm, sunny day in Moscow.

Negotiations continued on reducing strategic weapons, and Reagan continued to push forward his policies. In his speech to the United Nations on September 26, 1988, he said:

> The draft START treaty is a lengthy document, filled with bracketed language designating sections of disagreement between the two sides. But through this summer in Geneva, those brackets have diminished. There is every reason to believe this process can continue. I can tell this Assembly that it is highly doubtful such a treaty can be accomplished in a few months, but I can tell you a year from now is a possibility— more than a possibility. But we have no deadline. No agreement is better than a bad agreement.[8]

Summarizing progress in a statement on arms control negotiations on November 16, Reagan noted that while some agreements on reducing strategic weapons and verification regimes had been achieved, the Soviets continued to argue for the US abandonment of research on strategic defense as an alternative to mutual assured destruction:

> In START we are well on our way toward an agreement which will significantly reduce the levels of US and Soviet strategic nuclear arsenals. We have agreed on 50 percent reductions in deployed strategic forces . . . agreement has also been reached on the outlines of a verification regime. . . . Major areas of disagreement remain, including . . . Soviet attempts to link a START treaty to provisions that would cripple SDI. . . . SDI is our best hope for a safer world, one in which deterrence is increasingly based on defenses . . . rather than the threat of retaliation.[9]

On December 7, 1988, Gorbachev and Reagan met for a fifth time during Reagan's presidency, on Governor's Island in New York. Vice President George H. W. Bush was also present, but the two principals did most of the talking.

The meeting and lunch followed a speech Gorbachev gave at the United Nations, where he announced unilateral troop reductions of a half million, about 10 percent of the Soviet army, over two years. Six tank divisions would be withdrawn from East Germany, Czechoslovakia, and Hungary; they would be disbanded. That would include fifty thousand men and five thousand tanks. Altogether in the European part of the Soviet Union and the Eastern bloc "allies," the total reduction was ten thousand tanks, eighty-five hundred artillery systems, and eight hundred combat aircraft.

Gorbachev was apparently eager to continue the progress he and Reagan had made—not only on intermediate-range nuclear weapons, with the signing and ratification of the INF treaty, but also on the START treaty, where negotiators were continuing to work on a proposed 50 percent reduction in ballistic missiles. Gorbachev was being urged by advisors to reach out to President-elect George H. W. Bush; but Bush told Gorbachev on Governor's Island that he would "need a little time to review the issues."[10]

In 1988, the Politburo was still alive and well in Moscow, and the Soviet Union was still intact. But the Cold War was gone.

CHAPTER EIGHT

Freedom Won

In November 1989, the Berlin Wall fell. The Soviets did not intervene to quell unrest and prop up their Communist puppet leaders. Gorbachev had been urging East European Communist leaders to reform their systems along the lines of his own *perestroika* (economic and political reform), but they had not followed his lead.

Reagan had persuaded Gorbachev that the Soviet Union could not win the Cold War and dare not risk a nuclear war. It had taken a long time for Gorbachev to come around; he had needed part of the time to persuade his own military-industrial complex.

Gorbachev received the Nobel Peace Prize on May 4, 1990. The Soviet Union, once bent on world domination, with Western Europe an early target, had been persuaded that it could not compete economically, politically, or militarily with the United States and its Western allies, and therefore had to change. It was Ronald Reagan who accomplished that goal.

Gorbachev's opponents in the Soviet Union were dedicated to maintaining the Soviet empire. He successfully resisted an attempted coup in August 1991 as the Soviet Union, having lost its East European satellites, was itself dissolving into its fifteen so-called republics. Gorbachev stepped down on December 25, 1991, and the USSR officially dissolved on December 31, 1991.

Reagan did not crow about his success. He followed the policy he himself had written before his first summit meeting with his Soviet counterpart. "But let there be no talk of winners and losers. Even if we think we won, to say so would set us back in view of their inherent inferiority complex."[1]

In fact, Reagan awarded Gorbachev the first Ronald Reagan Freedom Award at the Reagan Presidential Library in 1992, not long after the Soviet leader was ousted from office. Mikhail Gorbachev was getting recognition—internationally and from Reagan personally—for his leadership.

Reagan, however, was still considered only a moderately successful president. As noted in Chapter 1, even in 1993, only 40 percent of US residents viewed him as a president who would go down in history as an outstanding or above-average president; and during the decade of the '90s, only 50 percent of respondents approved, in retrospect, of the job he had done in office.

In accepting the Reagan Freedom Award, Gorbachev said of himself and Reagan: "Together we covered perhaps the most difficult part of the road back from the edge of the abyss that the world was facing in the early 1980s."[2] As the next chapter records, Gorbachev would recall the 1985 Geneva summit as the significant beginning of their relationship.

Reagan noted on this occasion that he had wanted to meet the previous leaders of the Soviet Union—Brezhnev, Andropov, and Chernenko—"to tell them face-to-face that we had no intention of letting them win the arms race, so they had better get down to the business of joining us in ridding the world of nuclear weapons."[3] Reagan recalled his outreach to Gorbachev and their agreement to meet in Geneva.

And so one cold day in November of 1985, two men who held in their hands the power to end the world, began a journey. This journey would take us to Reykjavik, Moscow, Washington, and New York—taking the world from the threat of nuclear holocaust to the threshold of nuclear disarmament.[4]

"While reducing the threat of nuclear war remains my proudest accomplishment, I do not feel—and I know that Mikhail does not either—that our work is yet done. . . .

"It is true that the Cold War is over. Freedom won, as we always knew it would."[5]

CHAPTER NINE

Reagan and Gorbachev

He was a great man.
—*Mikhail Gorbachev, about Ronald Reagan, March 27, 2009*

On March 27, 2009, Mikhail Gorbachev addressed an audience at Eureka College, Ronald Reagan's alma mater. He spoke at the college during the day and at a dinner in Peoria, Illinois, in the evening. It was five years after Reagan's death, just over twenty years since Reagan had completed his two terms as president, and eighteen years since Gorbachev had resigned as president of the Soviet Union.

In his Eureka speech, Gorbachev recalled their first summit in Geneva:

> It was Reagan who was the first to say in Geneva that we need nuclear arms reduction and ultimately the elimination of nuclear weapons. He was a great president.

Two days after they first met, Gorbachev recounted, they made a joint statement of two or three pages. "I believe that the most important thing in that statement was the point that we made: A nuclear war cannot be won and must never be fought."[1]

Reagan had first used that statement in an April 1982 radio address to the American public. He used it again in his address in Tokyo to the Japanese Diet on November 11, 1983, also saying that "I know I speak for people everywhere when I say our dream is to see the day when nuclear weapons will be banished from the face of the earth."[2] At the end of his State of the Union address on January 25, 1984, he spoke directly to the Soviet people:

> Tonight, I want to speak to the people of the Soviet Union . . . there is only one sane policy, for your country and mine, to preserve our civilization in this modern age: A nuclear war cannot be won and must never be fought. The only value in our two nations possessing nuclear weapons is to make sure they will never be used.[3]

Reagan and Gorbachev signed the Intermediate-Range Nuclear Forces treaty, eliminating nuclear weapons of that type, in Washington, DC, on December 8, 1987. It was the first treaty to eliminate an entire class of nuclear weapons. Reagan and Gorbachev were also working on START—the Strategic Arms Reduction Treaty. The goal there was to reduce by 50 percent strategic nuclear weapons, including intercontinental ballistic missiles—those that could reach from Russia to the United States and vice versa. The two leaders made substantial progress, but the treaty was not ready for signature at the Moscow summit in 1988.

Nevertheless, Gorbachev also recalled in his Eureka speech how far he and Reagan had gotten on START at that point, giving the two of them the major credit for negotiating the treaty:

> . . . not only did we meet, not only did we exchange letters, we started talk to propose new agreements, and specifically we made proposals on the reductions of strategic nuclear weapons. And during the . . . Reagan-Gorbachev period, more than 75 percent of all issues in that treaty were agreed. . . .
>
> He was a great president, Gorbachev concluded.
>
> When all is said and done, he was a great man.[4]

Gorbachev had more to say about Reagan in a 2009 interview with *The Nation*, expressing his view that the Cold War ended well before the demise of the Soviet Union at the end of 1991:

If President Ronald Reagan and I had not succeeded in signing disarmament agreements and normalizing our relations in 1985–88, the
later developments would have been unimaginable. . . . the world could
not continue developing as it had, with the stark menace of nuclear
war ever present. . . . Something had to be done before we destroyed
each other.

Let me tell you something. George Shultz, Reagan's secretary of
state, came to see me two or three years ago. . . . I asked him: "Tell me,
George, if Reagan had not been president, who could have played his
role?" Shultz thought for a while, then said, "At that time there was no
one else. . . . in order to take these steps toward normalizing relations
with the Soviet Union and toward reducing nuclear armaments—there
was no one else who could have done that then."[5]

CHAPTER TEN

Nuclear Arsenals After Reagan, 1989–2012

The Bush I Years: 1989–93

Ronald Reagan handed George H. W. Bush the presidency on a platter. In 1988, Bush, Reagan's vice-president for eight years, defeated Democrat Michael Dukakis, former governor of Massachusetts, by a landslide, winning 53.4 percent of the popular vote.

Mikhail Gorbachev, the Soviet leader, was eager to continue with Reagan's successor the relationship he had developed with Reagan himself. Domestic reforms—*glasnost* (openness) and *perestroika* (economic and political reform)—were underway in the Soviet Union.

But Bush decided he needed a "prudent" review of foreign policy and national security policy, even though he had been in virtually every national security briefing and meeting Reagan had held in the last eight years.[1] The review was extensive. He did not re-engage with Gorbachev until their Malta summit in December 1989.

Reagan, meanwhile, took care to stay out of Bush's way. He was fully engaged in writing his own memoirs, speaking about the issues that concerned him on what he called the mashed-potato circuit, and spending time at the ranch he loved. He dedicated the Reagan Presidential Library on November 4, 1991. He awarded the first Ronald Reagan Freedom Award to Mikhail Gorbachev on May 4, 1992. On August 17 of that year, at the Republican National Convention, he gave what was to be his last major speech.

The reduction in total nuclear warheads during Bush's presidency was substantial. US warheads declined from 23,205 at the end of 1988—Reagan's last full year in office—to 13,708 at the end of 1992, the last full year of Bush's tenure. Soviet nuclear warheads declined from 28,288 to 21,200. The reductions included short-range nuclear weapons in Europe, the intermediate-range weapons eliminated by 1991 as a result of the Intermediate-Range Nuclear Forces treaty (846 US Pershing II and cruise missiles, and 1,846 Soviet missiles), and US reductions of 5,351 warheads on bombers, submarines, and intercontinental ballistic missiles to 990 comparable weapons for the Soviets.[2]

The strategic arms reduction treaty (START), on which Reagan and Gorbachev had made substantial progress, was finally signed in July 1991, over two years after Bush took office. The Soviets had not agreed to negotiate START independent of an agreement on missile defense (the Strategic Defense Initiative, or SDI) until September 22–23, 1989.

"We need to maintain and modernize our forces, nuclear and conventional," Bush said at the March 6, 1989, annual conference of the Veterans of Foreign Wars. In the same speech, he mentioned "vigorous pursuit of the Strategic Defense Initiative." He acknowledged Reagan's conviction and strategy in saying that "The fundamental lesson of this decade is simply this: strength secures the peace."[3]

At the commencement ceremony for the US Coast Guard Academy in New London, Connecticut, on May 24, 1989, Bush noted that deterrence was the central strategic tenet:

> The key to keeping the peace is convincing our adversaries that the cost of aggression against us or our allies is simply unacceptable. In today's world, nuclear forces are essential to deterrence. Our challenge is to protect those deterrent systems from attack.[4]

Bush supported SDI with both funds and words. Reagan had of course known that nuclear forces were an essential deterrent. But whereas Reagan emphasized that SDI held the potential for ultimately eliminating nuclear weapons, Bush flatly stated their need in Europe "as far as can be foreseen"[5]—an explicit acknowledgment of the importance of the nuclear deterrent in NATO given the vastly greater Soviet conventional forces.

On June 4, 1989, the Chinese government brutally suppressed pro-democracy demonstrations in Beijing's Tiananmen Square. The Berlin Wall fell on November 9 of that year, not long after Bush took office, unravelling Soviet control of Eastern Europe. On August 2, 1990, Iraq invaded Kuwait; five months later, a US-led coalition responded by launching the First Gulf War. At the end of 1991, the Soviet Union dissolved into its fifteen separate states, and Gorbachev resigned.

Bush and Russian President Boris Yeltsin signed the START II treaty on January 3, 1993, just days before Bush left office. It banned the use of multiple independently targetable re-entry vehicles on intercontinental ballistic missiles. The US Senate did not ratify it until 1996; the Russian Duma, not until 2000. The Russians withdrew from the treaty in 2002 and have since begun to rely on MIRVs again.

Bush lost the 1992 election to Bill Clinton. Although Bush's approval rating stood at an astonishing 91 percent after the Gulf War, that didn't last. A mild recession had begun in July 1990, ending ninety-two months of continuous economic expansion that began in November 1982, during the Reagan administration. Recovery did not commence again until March 1991. Worse, Bush had promised in his 1988 acceptance speech at the Republican National Convention, "Read my lips: no new taxes," a promise he broke. Asked about it by a reporter during a jogging session in October 1990, Bush looked back and said, "Read my hips."[6]

Bush also sought to fire and replace most of Reagan's appointees, depriving his administration of Republican strength and expertise developed during his predecessor's eight years in office.

The Clinton Years: 1993–2001

Clinton won the 1992 election with 43 percent of the popular vote to Bush's 37.5 percent; Ross Perot, who ran as an independent, picked up 18.9 percent, but no electoral votes. Clinton was re-elected in 1996 with 49.2 percent of the popular vote, defeating Senator Robert Dole, who got 40.7 percent, and Perot, with 8.4 percent.

US nuclear warheads under Clinton declined by another three thousand or so during his first two years in office, but then leveled off, stabilizing at ten thousand to eleven thousand. The Soviet decline was much greater—from 21,200 when Clinton took office to 11,188 in the year 2000. The Russians were working on meeting their obligations under the START I treaty and reducing tactical weapons.

Clinton emphasized the nuclear test-ban treaty and a new mission for the nation's nuclear weapons laboratories: "to continue to maintain the safety and reliability of our nuclear deterrent until all the nuclear weapons in the world are gone."[7] In an August 11, 1995, statement on the comprehensive nuclear test-ban treaty negotiations, he said, "As part of our national security strategy, the United States must and will retain strategic nuclear forces sufficient to deter any future hostile foreign leadership with access to strategic nuclear forces from acting against our vital interests and to convince it that seeking a nuclear advantage would be futile."[8]

Ronald Reagan made his last public speech on February 3, 1994. On April 27 of that year, he attended President Richard Nixon's funeral in Yorba Linda, California, the site of the Nixon Presidential Library. On November 5, in his well-known letter to "My Fellow Americans," he announced his formal retirement from public life.

The George W. Bush Years: 2001–09

George W. Bush was elected president on November 4, 2000, in a historically close race against former Senator Al Gore; Bush won the electoral college but got fewer popular votes than Gore, 47.9 percent to 48.4 percent. He was re-elected in 2004, beating John Kerry, then a senator from Massachusetts. The popular vote was Bush 50.7 percent, Kerry 48.3 percent.

In May 2001, early in his presidency—before the attack on the Manhattan twin towers of September 11, 2001—Bush spoke at the National Defense University, saying that "Cold War deterrence is no longer enough. . . . We need new concepts of deterrence that rely on both offensive and defensive forces. Deterrence can no longer be based solely on the threat of nuclear retaliation. Defenses can strengthen deterrence by reducing the incentive to proliferation."

Bush noted that the anti-ballistic missile (ABM) treaty of 1972 codified the vulnerability of the United States and the Soviet Union to

1937: *Love is on the Air*

One-sheet poster for Ronald Reagan's first film, in which he played a radio announcer. Warner Bros. Available on DVD.

1938: *Sergeant Murphy*

One-sheet poster. Warner Bros. Reagan played a Cavalry private who buys a horse—Sergeant Murphy—and enters it into a race. The horse earned more than Reagan did.

1938:   *Brother Rat*

One-sheet poster. Warner Bros. Reagan met Jane Wyman, who became his first wife, while working on this movie.

Licensed by Warner Bros. Entertainment Inc. All rights reserved.

1939: *Code of the Secret Service*

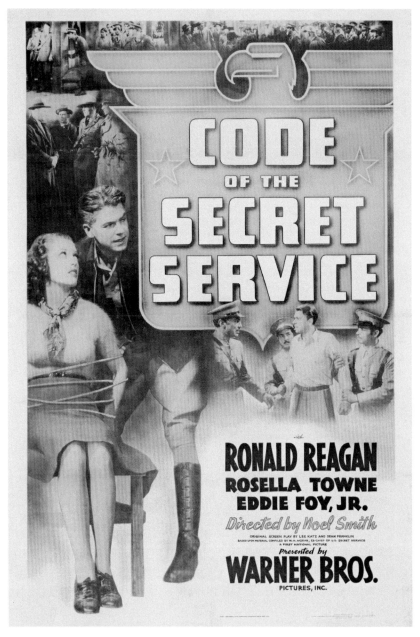

One-sheet poster, Warner Bros./First National. Available on DVD.
Although Reagan considered this a poor film, it was the inspiration for the
career choice of Secret Service Agent Jerry Parr, who protected Reagan
during the 1981 assassination attempt.

1939: *Smashing the Money Ring*

One-sheet poster for Reagan's third film as Brass Bancroft, crime-fighter.
Warner Bros. Available on DVD.

Licensed by Warner Bros. Entertainment Inc. All rights reserved.

1940: *Murder in the Air*

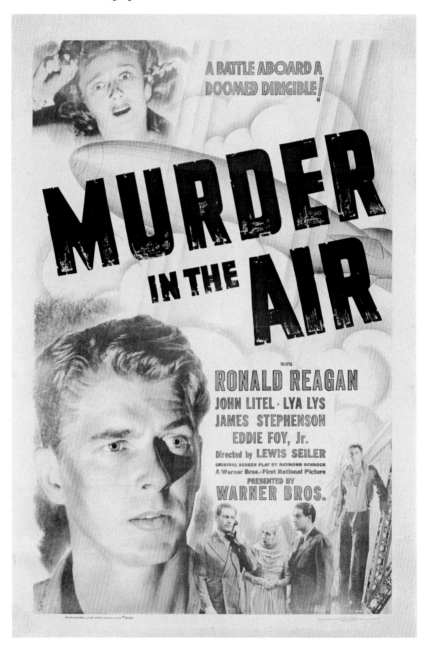

One-sheet poster. Reagan, in his fourth film as Brass Bancroft, wields a new weapon capable of shooting down airplanes in flight. Warner Bros. Available on DVD.

One-sheet poster. Warner Bros. Reagan played George Gipp in this football movie. He got the part only after showing the producer some photos of himself playing football at Eureka College.

1941: *International Squadron*

One-sheet poster. Warner Bros. Reagan played heroic pilot Jimmy Grant
helping the British in the days before the US entered World War II.
Licensed by Warner Bros. Entertainment Inc. All rights reserved.

1942: *Kings Row*

One-sheet poster. Warner Bros. Available on DVD. A favorite film of
Reagan's and one of his best performances, in which he delivered the line that
would become the title of his first autobiography, "Where's the rest of me?"

1943: *This Is the Army*

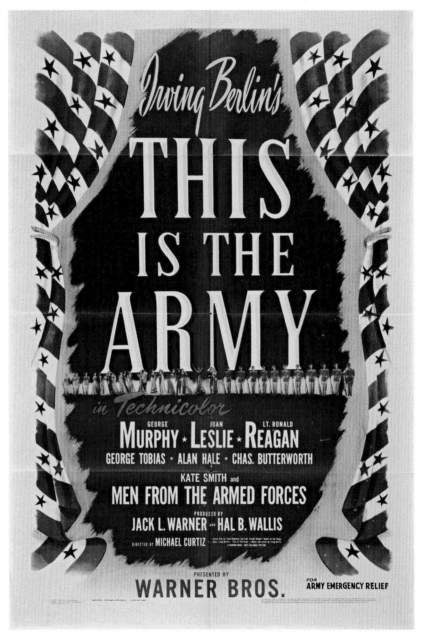

One-sheet poster. Reagan, serving in World War II as an Army lieutenant, was assigned to Warner Bros. on temporary duty to make this movie. All profits went to Army Emergency Relief. Reagan earned only his Army pay. Warner Bros. Available on DVD.

1949: *The Hasty Heart*

One-sheet poster. Warner Bros. Available on DVD. Reagan found post-war
England, where the filming was done, dreary and overly bureaucratic.

1950: *Bedtime for Bonzo*

One-sheet poster. Universal International. Available on DVD. Reagan said of the film, "I fought a losing battle with a scene stealer—a chimpanzee."

1951:   *Storm Warning*

One-sheet poster. Warner Bros. Available on DVD. Reagan played a county prosecutor who battles the Ku Klux Klan.

One-sheet poster. Universal. Available on DVD. A Western in which Reagan, as Marshal Frame Johnson, fights corruption and restores order in a frontier town.

1954: *Prisoner of War*

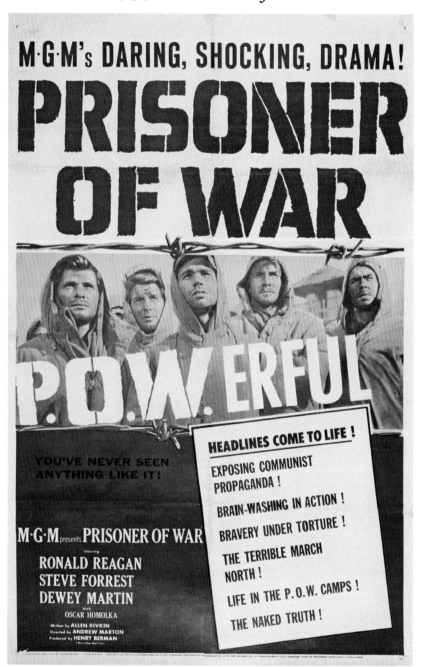

One-sheet poster. Metro-Goldwyn-Mayer. Reagan played a prisoner in a
Korean prison camp run by the Soviets.

1957: *Hellcats of the Navy*

One-sheet poster. Morningside Productions/Columbia Pictures. Reagan and his wife, Nancy Davis, were the leads, their only feature film together.

Courtesy of Columbia Pictures. All rights reserved.

nuclear retaliation in the event of an attack by either side; US nuclear weapons were also the counter to the 1.5 million Soviet troops stationed near or in Eastern Europe. But the threat was now from missiles in the hands of some of the world's least responsible states willing to use terror and blackmail. "We should leave behind the constraints of an ABM Treaty that perpetuates a relationship based on distrust and mutual vulnerability," Bush said.[9] The United States withdrew from the treaty in June 2002, after giving the required six months' notice of its intent on December 13, 2001. By 2004, a rudimentary missile defense was in place, and Bush would later talk about its importance.[10]

On May 24, 2002, Bush and Russian president Vladimir Putin signed the Moscow Strategic Offensive Reductions Treaty (SORT). The treaty came into force on June 1, 2003, after both sides ratified it. Under SORT, each of the parties agreed to limit its nuclear arsenals to between 1,700 and 2,200 "operationally deployed" warheads. The treaty had no verification provisions and did not require the destruction of warheads.

In June 2004, President Bush directed the US military to cut in half its stockpile of both deployed and reserve nuclear weapons by 2012,[11] a reduction of US nuclear warheads to just over 50 percent of the 2001 total.

At the end of 2008, the United States had 5,273 warheads, the Russians 5,576. At the US Military Academy at West Point, on December 9, 2008, as his presidency was winding down, Bush said that the US actions sent a clear message to the world: "We'll reduce our reliance on nuclear weapons while keeping America's strategic deterrent unchallenged."[12]

The Barack Obama Years: 2000–

Senator Barack Obama prevailed over Senator John McCain in the election of 2008, winning 52.9 percent of the popular vote to McCain's 45.7 percent. During the campaign, both candidates spoke out in favor of eliminating nuclear weapons as an ultimate goal. This goal had been articulated in a December 2007 *Wall Street Journal* op-ed authored by four of the nation's most respected senior statesmen, two Republicans and two Democrats: George P. Shultz, Henry Kissinger, former Senator Sam Nunn, and William Perry.

In a speech in Prague, Obama talked about America's commitment to seek the peace and security of a world without nuclear weapons:

> This goal will not be reached quickly—perhaps not in my lifetime. . . . As long as these weapons exist, the United States will maintain a safe, secure, and effective arsenal to deter any adversary, and guarantee that defense to our allies. . . .[13]

Obama and Russian President Dmitri Medvedev negotiated the new START treaty, signed on April 8, 2010. It was ratified by the US Senate on December 22, 2010, and by the Russian Duma one month later. In his November 20, 2010, radio address urging ratification, Obama noted that "This treaty is rooted in a practice that dates back to Ronald Reagan. . . . 'Trust but verify.'" Although the treaty called for further reduction of nuclear weapons, the two sides did not reach agreement on missile defense.

Obama was elected to a second term in 2012, defeating former Massachusetts governor Mitt Romney while winning 51.1 percent of the popular vote and 332 electoral votes.

By the end of 2010, the United States had five thousand nuclear warheads, the Russians 4,692. At the end of 2012, the numbers were 4,472 for the Russians and still about five thousand for the United States.[14]

Nuclear arsenals have been dramatically reduced since Ronald Reagan persuaded Mikhail Gorbachev that a nuclear war was indeed unwinnable and should never be fought. The United States and Russia continue to hold about 90 percent of the world's nuclear arsenals.

CHAPTER ELEVEN

The Reagan Legacy

The world is substantially different today than it was during the Cold War. The nuclear arsenals of the United States and Russia are far smaller than they were at the peak of the Soviet Union's buildup in the mid-1980s, and missile defense against short-range and intermediate-range missiles is coming into increasing use. Reagan's dream of a world without nuclear weapons has not been realized, but Reagan set out the goal and proposed a way to get there—a shared defense against missile attacks that would make nuclear weapons obsolete.

The original five nuclear-weapons states—the United States, the Soviet Union (now Russia), the United Kingdom, France, and China—have increased in number to nine. The other four are Israel (although it does not admit to having nuclear weapons), Pakistan, India, and North Korea. The total inventory (some of it in storage or nonstrategic) is about 16,400 warheads.[1] Iran is considered likely to have a nuclear weapons program underway; Libya gave up its program in 2004; and South Africa gave up both its program and its weapons materiel in the early 1990s.

Hans Kristensen and Robert Norris, the long-time authors of the periodic estimates of nuclear stockpiles regularly published in the Nuclear Notebook of the *Bulletin of the Atomic Scientists*, have serious words of caution about the numbers. "Excessive secrecy," they write, "prevents the public from knowing the exact number of nuclear weapons in the world."[2] Some countries don't provide basic information on their arsenals. One of the authors' noteworthy estimates is that China's stockpile has, they believe, surpassed that of Great Britain.[3] The authors also point out that arms control agreements usually do not require destruction of warheads, and estimates exclude non-deployed and non-strategic warheads. Although the total warhead count has gone down, nations continue to upgrade and modernize their nuclear arsenals.[4]

The Legacy of Reykjavik

Twenty years after Ronald Reagan and Mikhail Gorbachev met at Reykjavik, Iceland, to pursue their agenda of reducing the threat of nuclear war, George Shultz and Sidney Drell[5] convened a conference on the implication of that summit meeting, where the leaders of the world's two superpowers first considered the possibility of totally eliminating nuclear weapons. The nuclear warheads of the two superpowers had already been dramatically reduced to fewer than ten thousand on each side. Senators Sam Nunn and Richard Lugar had headed an effort, begun in 1991 through the Soviet Threat Reduction Act, to provide funds and a program to secure and dismantle the weapons and weapons materiel in the states of the former Soviet Union.

Shultz and Drell put together a remarkable group of experts in politics, technology, and international affairs. In spite of the accomplishments of the Reagan years and the results of the arms reduction treaties that followed, other considerations concerned the participants: proliferation, terrorism, rogue states. Martin Anderson reviewed Reagan's commitment to a world free of nuclear weapons. Max Kampelman, one of the major US arms-control negotiators during the Cold War, told the group that in his view President Reagan was correct in urging a zero objective for nuclear weapons. "What we need today," he said, "is a 'Reagan-esque' initiative designed to enlarge the diplomatic canvas so that all nations can be convinced that the global elimination of nuclear weapons is in their national interest."[6]

Although Kampelman had earlier tried to engage the George W. Bush administration on the issue of abolishing nuclear weapons, he had gotten no response. And some months before the conference on the Reykjavik summit, former Senator Sam Nunn, Shultz, Drell, William J. Perry (former secretary of defense), and others met to consider whether the goal of eliminating nuclear weapons would further efforts to reduce nuclear dangers.[7] Nunn and his colleagues at the Nuclear Threat Initiative had long been concerned about concrete steps that needed to be taken to reduce the nuclear threat.

While the conference was still being planned, Shultz approached Henry Kissinger about the goal of eliminating nuclear weapons. The result—after repeated consultations about details—was an op-ed, published in *The Wall Street Journal* on January 4, 2007, a few months after the conference actually occurred, entitled "A World Free of Nuclear Weapons."[8] The piece was signed by Shultz, Perry, Kissinger, and Nunn—two Republicans, two Democrats, two secretaries of state, a secretary of defense, and a former senator prominent in national defense circles.

Mikhail Gorbachev wrote in the same newspaper on January 31, 2007, "As someone who signed the first treaties on real reductions in nuclear weapons, I feel it is my duty to support their call for urgent action."[9]

In the presidential election of 2008, both candidates—Barack Obama and John McCain—supported the idea of abolishing nuclear weapons.

President Obama spoke on the issue of nuclear weapons in Prague on April 6, 2009, emphasizing not only the goal but also steps along the way—and the importance of maintaining deterrence. Obama met with Shultz, Perry, Nunn, and Kissinger in the Oval Office on May 19, 2009, and again in 2010.

All those men and their efforts stood in the shadow of Ronald Reagan. As Nunn said later, "If the world makes it to the nuclear-free mountaintop, we will have President Reagan to thank for inspiring our climb." Without Reagan's vision of the importance and possibility of making the world safe from nuclear weapons, the vision of a Cold Warrior who saw the possibility of moving beyond that war, they would not have come together to do what they did.

Ballistic Missile Defense

Reagan's vision of a world free of nuclear weapons was grounded in his goal of a defense against those weapons. Reagan walked out of the Reykjavik summit because the Soviets refused to negotiate unless the United States agreed to confine its research on ballistic missile defense to the laboratory.

At the time that Reagan proposed the Strategic Defense Initiative (SDI)—a research program on ballistic missile defense—the United States had no defenses against such missiles in place. It had shut down its only defensive system—the Safeguard system at Grand Forks, North Dakota, which protected a missile field—as ineffective in response to an all-out Soviet attack. By contrast, the Soviet Union had a system to shoot down missiles aimed at Moscow.

SDI was funded during the Reagan and George H. W. Bush administrations but virtually mothballed during the Clinton years. Thus there is no system that, as Reagan envisioned, could "hit those missiles as they came out of their silos,"[10] a system that would have countered the threat of an all-out Soviet attack. Since the end of the Cold War, such an attack or an invasion of Europe by Russia has been of less immediate concern than the threats from smaller states and terrorist groups.

Under President George W. Bush, the United States withdrew from the ABM treaty limiting missile defense in 2002. Research efforts on more limited defensive systems have continued, and some are in place. But a space-based defense against nuclear missiles has not been developed.

The United States now operates two ground-based, mid-course defense-interceptor sites, one at Vandenberg Air Force Base in California and the other in Alaska. It also has, based on navy ships, the AEGIS ballistic-missile defense system, which President Obama favored over a ground-based system in Poland. In addition, the

THAAD (terminal high-altitude area defense) system became operational in some locations in 2008. The PAC-3 (Patriot Advanced Capability) systems also provide terminal air defense, that is, defense against missiles as they come in to hit their targets.

India, France, the United Kingdom, Italy, Israel, South Korea, Japan, and the Republic of China (Taiwan) are either working on or have developed missile defense systems, often in cooperation with the United States. China and Russia also have such systems in place.

Martin Anderson's Interview with Ronald Reagan, Los Angeles, July 25, 1989

Transcript

Martin Anderson interviewed Ronald Reagan on July 25, 1989, at Reagan's office in Los Angeles. Reagan had concluded his eight years as president only six months before—on January 20—and was working on his memoirs. Anderson had served on Reagan's presidential campaign staff in 1976 and 1980, and also as his assistant for policy development. On this occasion, he was gathering information for an update to his book, Revolution, *published in 1988.*

The interview lasted an hour, and this transcript was made from tapes recorded while it was underway. Some of the exchanges, or portions of them, have been quoted in other sections of this book.

Anderson: A little over ten years ago, I went with you to the ranch in Santa Barbara. You had an interview with [political commentator] Bill Moyers, and he challenged you. I remember him saying—this was when you were just thinking about running for president, in 1979— "You know some people will say you're too old, you're too reluctant, you're not hungry enough to pay the price of becoming president, and you're out of touch."

You answered, "Well, I don't want to be president in the sense that I want to live in the White House, but I want, I want the chance . . . there are things that I think can be done." But now looking back, ten years later, did you get done some of the big things you wanted to get done?

Reagan: Oh, yes. Didn't get them all, there's some things that really haunt me to this day, and I'll sit around the mashed-potato circuit and they'll find out up at the [Bohemian] Grove Saturday I'm still talking about it. But when I think back, the one thing as I look back and think maybe was different from many who have taken that position was I had a plan, I had a program. I really was, as I said there, concerned about something that I thought had to happen in government. And we were coming into a time when America was being told, even by its leaders then, to lower their sights, that never again would we have the lush days that we'd had. We found out that on any given day 50 percent of our military aircraft couldn't fly for lack of spare parts and our ships couldn't leave harbor for that or lack of crew. We had the double-digit inflation, we had the double-digit unemployment, and we were really in economic recession, which we were being told was really what we must get used to, that this was going to be—likely to be—the way things were, you know.

I had some strong beliefs. One of them was that . . . a tax cut was necessary to give the government the revenue it should have. If you look at history, every time we cut the tax rates, the total income went up. And so that was part of the economic summit. I was very concerned about the reawakening, I call it a spiritual reawakening, a reawakening of people's pride in country and so forth. Do you know that at that time 94 percent of the enlisted personnel in our military were high school drop-outs? Today about that same percentage are high school graduates. It's the highest percentage that we've ever had in our military, in the history of the military. So I think that maybe it was by virtue of having been governor and facing some of the problems and seeing that they could be turned around and changed. That was. . . .

Anderson: Let me ask you this for a minute. You sure got those things done in spades. This month is the most remarkable month that's gone unremarked in the press. It's the 81st straight month of economic recovery. That makes it not only the longest peacetime expansion in history, but it even now surpasses the World War II record which was 80 months, but we still have to catch the Vietnam-wartime expansion, which was 106. And if you look at what's going on with nuclear arms reduction, I think almost everyone will agree that most Americans are a lot prouder than they were ten years ago.

But there's something curious going on out there right now. There's a new book out by Bob Schieffer, called *The Acting President.* I spent an hour debating him yesterday morning up in San Francisco on television. There's a lot of articles starting to come out now. The theme of this whole book—believe it or not—is that the last eight years had nothing to do with ideology or principles, that you had no plan, no program, that you made no decisions, that everything was done in your name by a few people in spite of the bad things that people like Shultz and Meese and characters like that did. It's an extraordinary fairy tale.

Because I remember 10 years ago when you talked about your plan, and I guess the question is, how do you feel about that and are you going to deal directly with some of things in your memoirs to set the record straight?

Reagan: Yes [laughing softly, looking at book cover], CBS news chief, Washington correspondent, and Gary Paul Gates, co-author, *The Palace Guard.* How the hell could they say this?

Anderson: Here's the summary. I challenged him directly, and I said, "You know, that's just not true." And he just smiled and looked at it.

Reagan: What was his response?

Anderson: He said, "Well, that's your opinion."

Reagan: Does he quote us?

Anderson: Well, most of the stuff in the book is second- and third-hand stuff from previous books, especially Don Regan and Mike Deaver's books and Larry Speakes' book. But then he did do interviews with John Sears and Deaver and Speakes. Those are the main ones.

Reagan: Well, what did Deaver say to them, for example?

Anderson: He didn't say much, it was toward the end. I think Mike was just kind of disappointed and sad these days. But the reason I bring this up is that there really is a movement out there in the media and the intellectual world: a lot of people are very upset at how successful you were. It's beginning to happen.

I also remember you saying, I know you mentioned it a number of times: a) you never cared what the historians thought about you and b) I remember you once telling me there was no limit to what a man could get done if he didn't care who got credit for it. But let me ask you this, now that you've finished your presidency, don't you think it's important that the historians get it straight? Because there are a lot of young people coming along who don't know what happened, and the story that's coming out now is that a) nothing much happened and b) you had nothing to do with what did happen.

Reagan: Oh, for heaven's sakes. Well now, the funny thing, Marty, is [that] in every kind of meeting and places where I go and speak—and good Lord, I've done a dozen speeches already and more since I've been out there—but going through the receiving line—and these are knowledgeable people, business people, because some of these are actually business conventions that I'm addressing—I can almost say in advance what *they're* going to say. They come up and take my hand. They start thanking me for these eight years and what has been accomplished. And then some of them will tell about where they were eight years ago and where they are now, and some of it really is a success story, in a sense, that they're telling. So the people feel that way.

Well, I will have a book coming up. The first book obviously is one of my speeches and so forth, but then the other one is going to be on my views of the White House and so forth. That'll be another year or so before it comes out.

But good lord, don't the numbers tell the story?

Anderson: The Schieffer book is interesting. There is no mention of the number of months of economic growth, about what happened to the tax rate, there's no mention of the 18,510,000 jobs that have been created. It's just not talked about.

Reagan: Well, that's the amazing thing that they do that. And then some things like on a whole different subject—things like Grenada. We received a midnight phone call from the several other Caribbean island states and they said, from their vantage point, that Grenada had been taken over by a communist government. And they thought they were next; in fact, they were *convinced* they were next. And they didn't have the manpower—they would provide what manpower they had—but they couldn't do it without us providing [most of] the manpower.

Well, I think it was the only secret that we ever managed to keep in the White House—48 hours—the chiefs of staff—we didn't even tell our press section, and then finally on the night that our forces set sail, because the thing that had to be kept so quiet was because Cuba was so much closer. If the Cubans felt that we were going to come, we would have met some solid Cuban troops there on the shore. And so it was a secret. And then that night, once they were on their way with only a few hours left before they'd land, and then we called the leadership of the Congress over to the White House and told them what was going on. And, um, Tip O'Neill was kind of grumpy about the whole thing, and yet they didn't quite know just how the hell to react. And, as you know, it was going to be over in 48 hours and we had a few casualties but we certainly saved 800 young medical students—Americans who were there at that medical college. I had the thrill—a short time later after it was all over—of standing on the South Lawn and seeing a mix of several hundred of those and a few hundred of the forces that had gone in there. And literally to see these students drop to their knees in front of these soldiers [soft chuckle] and—

Anderson: One of them kissed the ground, if I remember correctly.

Reagan: That's right, yes. And then to make later a trip down there. And you know, we're so used to having "Yankee Go Home" printed on the walls and everything, and it's just unbelievable the banners that were up across the street, and the population . . . well, one of the things that we uncovered, and speaking of the press, and this I guess is what I started, and I don't want to take up too much time to tell, we came back with all the papers and things that we had confiscated; things like the Cuban embassy.

The walls of the embassy were hollow and filled with weapons. The Cuban workers who were building the airport were all military personnel temporarily in the cities doing this. But the papers and everything we put in the hanger at Andrews Air Force Base. Now here were Soviet documents revealing the plans that this was only the beginning and then the other islands were to go and everything. And all of this we made available to anyone, the press or anyone could go in there and read this collection of documents. And you never saw a word of it in the press; I don't know that they ever even went over.

Anderson: Let me ask you another question. You've been out of office for six months now. How many reporters have asked to interview you about the accomplishments of your administration?

Reagan: Not very many.

Anderson: Coming back to this theme that people are trying to play now, my recollection is that you know you always encouraged a lot of different views, but you always reserved making the decision for yourself. One of the charges in the book here is that, for example, "His decision to concentrate White House policy on tax cuts and defense spending," and by "his" they mean Jimmy Baker. Now I remember sitting in on many meetings with Baker and he was absolutely scrupulous about presenting options to you, [but] you made the decisions. I know it sounds silly to ask the question, but is that the way you remember it?

Reagan: Good lord, yes. It was the way I had always done it as governor and, if you will remember, I kept a thing that I coined when I was governor and that was I did not want to hear the political ramifications of any issue we were discussing. I wanted to hear from whoever thought it was bad, whoever thought it was good. And nothing except what would be the effect on the people—what was good for the people was made the basis for the decision. And if anyone started to raise the political thing, I shut 'em up.

Anderson: I guess I can't understand how you can stay so calm about it. Because I got really upset yesterday morning.

Reagan: Well, I suppose I would have, too, with this character. By golly. How the hell they can say the things that? The thing that I joked about was, you know, the minute our program started it was "Reaganomics."

Anderson: That's right.

Reagan: But when it succeeded, they stopped calling it Reaganomics. They were thinking, all the time they were calling it that, that it was a great big thing that was going to collapse.

Anderson: One of the places they're getting this stuff from is Stockman's book and Regan's book, which have had a terrifically wide circulation, and some of the charges in them were kind of outrageous.

Reagan: Oh, Stockton's [sic]. I read his and I couldn't believe it. Because, you know, his having been a member of Congress and all, I can remember at meetings when he was at OMB, when we would be talking about various budget cuts and so forth, that he would interrupt and say, "I'll tell you now, if you try to get that and put that in the budget, the budget will be dead on arrival when it gets there." And he'd talk us out of it. Then he writes in a book as if he was the only one that was proposing cuts and we were the spendthrifts.

Anderson: I know. Looking back on it now, I remember when Stockman's article came out in the *Atlantic Monthly* and you gave him a second chance. Have you had second thoughts about that second chance?

Reagan: Yes, I have. Why, he came in and he was so open. And he apologized so abjectly and said that the big picture he had painted—he didn't say "I didn't say these things"—he said this man was kind of a confidante and a good friend and he felt that he could give his views to him but that this man was never going to reveal them and then he claimed that this was the result of it, and so forth. Well, what the hell. [Soft laugh]

Anderson: Let me ask you this then, I think a lot of young people would be interested in this, I think—watching you and other presidents. One of the most difficult things to do is to decide what you're going to do in the eight or ten hours a day you have to do it in. There are so many things you could get into, so many decisions you have to make. How did you go about making those priorities? How did you decide what you were going to do every day, how did you go about making decisions?

Reagan: Well, only now and then was there some kind of a decision that had a date by which you had to do it coming up. Most of them would be battled out there, and every time, I, as you know from experience . . . I would predict my decision, and I would take what I heard with me. Now once in a great while there were times when there was so much right on both sides that I would call another meeting and say I wasn't satisfied yet that I had all the information I needed to make the decision.

But that wasn't too often. The other [times], I would just take it and sit down with it. Sometimes it would be a thing which I could give my views to some individual, like the chief of staff or something, and tell him what I thought. And really, what I was doing it for was not to take their advice but to find out from someone else whether they could actually give a specific rebuttal. . . . And most often there wouldn't be any rebuttal. They wouldn't be able to counter what I said was my belief.

Anderson: That reminds me of something else. When I read the reports of your book, one of the things they mentioned again in there was that you kept a personal diary in the White House.

Reagan: See those three red books over there?

Anderson: Yes.

Reagan: That's part of it. We've been looking up something on the first administration. Those three red books lying there are the diaries of the first administration.

Anderson: Well, I know there are some people who are real nervous about those books. [Laughter] The question that I've heard people saying is "When did he find time to do it? How did he do it? How did he go about doing this?" because the assumption was that, you know, you're kind of lazy, you didn't do much in the government, let alone put in full time being the president of the United States—[yet] you still wrote a personal diary. How did you do that?

Reagan: Every night—

Anderson: Every night?

Reagan: —when I came up at the end of the day. Sometimes I'd have to make kind of little notes because of my memory. You see, what started all of this was the governorship. After eight years, Nancy and I both found ourselves—I don't think it was age—really unable to say did this happen in the first administration or the second. And this was when the other thing that happened [election to the presidency] that we both said, now we've learned our lesson. We'll keep a diary. And she kept a diary, and I kept a diary.

Anderson: She's kept one too?

Reagan: Oh, yes. Just her own activities and so forth. But sometimes during the day, I also found that [the memory problem] wasn't just me. We'd start the day with a staff meeting, and then there would be a National Security Council Meeting. And a few times I found myself really racking my brain, and as the rest of the day went on, I said, what the hell did we talk about? Well, I, fearing that it was just me, I said to these younger people a couple of times, at the end of the day, do you remember what we talked about in the morning? And they said no.

Anderson: That's been my experience. If I didn't have some notes to be able to refer to, I would not be able to recall what happened.

Reagan: Well, I used to, every once in a while during the day, just make a little key line that would titillate my memory then. And these weren't in great, full detail, because I figured that if I put enough there, then my memory would take care of it, and I'd have that to go by. So in other words, I didn't go word-by-word of everything. There are very few entries in [the diary] that are more than a page.

Anderson: Did you write on the long yellow legal pads as usual?

Reagan: [Low laughter] I'm so glad to have them. And then, I found out, with them, and here with this book that's being done, being commissioned with Lindsey, I suddenly discovered that I was having something of that same [memory] problem. So, I had to go [to the diaries]. I have just finished reading the entire set.

Anderson: How many volumes do you have?

Reagan: I think it's about six. I can tell you exactly in a minute. I'll just take one quick look. I have these three out looking some things up. These are from—no, by golly, it's five. Five books.

Anderson: Let me ask you another question. There was something you did that was very unusual, for eight years. And not many people paid much attention to it. But you gave the vice president extraordinary opportunity, and if I remember right, you had lunch with him almost every single week. A private lunch, which comes to something like over 350 lunches, maybe more than that.

Reagan: The day was Thursday.

Anderson: Can you tell us now what kinds of things you talked about? Did you just sit and eat, or did you talk policy, or—

Reagan: Oh, we talked about things and not always decision types of things. We talked about things that were going on. Because, as you know, just as I did with the lieutenant governor as governor, I did with the vice president: I made him a part of the administration, not sitting on the side and waiting for me to get sick. So he was a part of everything that we did.

For example, the first thing, I assigned him to chair a task force to see how many federal regulations could be eliminated. This was a part of leading to the federalism I wanted. That was another thing we had to correct. We had to get back to where we are a federation of sovereign states. And for years and years, due to the Congress, they've been whittling away trying to make the states just administrative districts of the federal government. And I made him challenge that.

And when that task force's report came in, the result was the book that we left that lists the federal regulations is only half as big as it was when we got there. And we estimate that the savings in record keeping and paperwork, by either individuals or local government or states and so forth, that there has been a saving of 600 million man-hours a year.

Anderson: Would it be fair to say, given that extraordinary number of meetings of private one-on-ones with the vice president, that looking back on it he was probably your main advisor?

Reagan: Well, I have to say this—

Anderson: On a whole range of problems.

Reagan: I think [he] recognized his position as such that he didn't attempt to volunteer something and say "You ought to be doing. . . . " No, he wouldn't do that at all.

Anderson: But if you asked for his advice, he certainly would have.

Reagan: Yes. But I always noticed—did *you* ever notice?—that in the cabinet meetings, in there with everyone else there, he never, never spoke up? He'd answer a question directly if I asked him. But I still think he was a part of everything we were doing.

Anderson: He seems to be doing pretty well now.

Reagan: Yes. And I think he took abuse for a while because he was the first vice president in 135 years to succeed a president of his own party. Now, most people expect a president, well, just like what I did, I said I came in with a plan. So, yes, there was a, it was very easy at first to get excited, I mean [get] people excited, because, boom, you get a great big tax reform and so forth [that] you're going to do.

Anderson: Let me go back to that plan [you mentioned], because I think that when the historians look back at these eight years they may say that the most important thing you achieved was nuclear disarmament with the Soviet Union. And I remember back in 1976, at the convention in Kansas City, when President Ford called you down, waved you down from up in the balcony. And you made a speech that night, it was off the cuff, extemporaneous, and, let me just quote you a sentence from that speech. You talked about the great challenge we face, and that challenge, you said, was that we lived in a world in which the great powers have poised, aimed at each other, the horrible missiles of destruction that can in a matter of minutes arrive in each other's country and destroy virtually the civilized world we live in.

It seems to me that over the past thirteen years you have continually come back to that theme—what can we do about reducing the threat of nuclear war. I just wonder, did you have a plan all along? Was the defense buildup tied to that? Was SDI tied to that? In other words, was the defense buildup and SDI part of the plan to do something about nuclear war or were they separate?

Reagan: No, they were together. First of all, we inherited the Mutual Assured Destruction, the MAD, policy. I thought that was the most ridiculous thing I had ever seen, that you could stand there, like two guys with guns pointed at each other's heads and cocked and thinking that neither one of them will take a chance and pull on that trigger. But to have the power to destroy, literally, the civilized world, and it would only take somebody pushing a button to launch that, because if they launched theirs first, you know that ours would be on their way even though we'd be blown up too.

So one of the early things I did was that I called a meeting of the Chiefs of Staff in the cabinet room. And I said, look, every weapon that's ever been created in the world has resulted in a defense, a defensive weapon, the sword and later the shield, and so forth. And I said, isn't it with our technology possible that we could produce a system that could hit those missiles as they came out of their silos, using space, whatever? Well, they kind of huddled for a minute, and then they came back and they said could you give us a couple of days on that? And I said yes.

In a couple of days they came back and said, yes, we think it is worthwhile. We think with today's technology we can develop something of that kind that would virtually make them obsolete. Because no one would want to press the button if you knew that only a half a dozen of the weapons would ever get through, leaving us able then to retaliate. So I said, all right, we start, go to it. And so we started that plan. And to the point that at my first meeting with Gorbachev, he jumped on that. And I said, that is not a bargaining chip. And told him, look, if we're successful with that, what we're doing, I'll tell you what my own view is, we should share it with you and with the world. Because all of us know how to make those missiles now, so if we do just say we're going to eliminate them, and we eliminate them, we would still have to live with the thought that someday along could come a man like Hitler and make them again, and blackmail the world. So I said this is like we did back in 1925 when we all met in Switzerland and decided against chemical warfare. And I said we all agreed to do away with them, and we all kept our gas masks.

Anderson: Did he agree with your basic thrust?

Reagan: For one thing, he said, "I don't believe you"—that I would share.

So what is obvious, what his attempt was, and several times later he did it, his attempt was I think to find some way to get—by reducing arms and everything—to get us to give up on it. But I've also suspected, and I think there's evidence to bear this out, that the Soviet Union scientists were exploring the same thing, only they don't have our technology yet and couldn't do it. But I spoke a line, when I addressed the British Parliament and I think some other government bodies in other countries: "A nuclear war cannot be won and must never be fought." And the biggest thrill I had was in a meeting a few years later than that in our country, when Mr. Gorbachev's foreign secretary, Shevardnadze, when he, speaking on his own, said "A nuclear war can never be won and must never be fought."

Anderson: Good line.

Reagan: [Laughter] In the past, in our summit meetings with the Soviet leaders, we were always trying to get some agreement out of them by making concessions, and I came in determined that the only way to peace was through strength. When I called them the "Evil Empire" in a public speech, I did it on purpose. I wanted them to know that we saw them for what they were, and as I said to him in one meeting, one of our earliest meetings, to Gorbachev—I told him it was someone else's line—that we didn't mistrust each other because we were armed, but [were] armed because we mistrusted each other.

Anderson: Some of my conservative friends think that you flip flopped and changed your mind—that at one point you called them the Evil Empire and the next thing you know you were dealing with them and negotiating with them. And I tried to explain, I think you had something else in mind.

Reagan: Yes, because I said to him [Gorbachev] then, after I said that, I said "It's not enough—you and I, engaged in dealings here trying to reduce the weaponry that we have. Why don't we start trying to reduce what causes the mistrust between us? But I will tell you now, we can continue to disarm or we can continue the arms race, and I'll tell you now, you can't win the arms race. There is no way."

Anderson: You told him that directly?

Reagan: Yes sir. I said, there's no way that we're going to allow you, or anyone else, to maintain supremacy over the United States of America.

Anderson: Well, he's smarter than I thought he was.

Reagan: He is the first Russian leader since the Revolution who has ever agreed to a treaty in which they would destroy weapons they already have, the INF treaty. Always before, they would make treaties about how many they would come to, but never were they willing to destroy a weapon. And now you hear him offering to destroy them all.

And I made it plain to him also that in the destroying of nuclear weapons, this was going to have to be tied to the conventional [weapons], because they had superiority and the only thing we had to respond to that superiority was nuclear. So we weren't going to sit here and join them in a nuclear disarmament at the expense of leaving them with a 10 to 1 advantage in tanks and artillery.

Anderson: I don't know if anyone has ever asked you this, but I've often wondered: it seemed to me that probably the toughest thing about being president was that you had the responsibility of ultimately deciding whether or not to retaliate in case the Soviets attacked us. How did you think about that? Did you have any contingency plan? Did you ever think and say, my God, what if they do? You know, what will we do? Will we just sit here and accept the missiles; will we launch a retaliatory attack? How do you deal with that?

Reagan: One of the difficulties in bargaining with them was most of their nuclear force was land based, missiles in silos. Ours was a triad—missiles in silos, nuclear submarines and so forth out there and with weapons that had to be tracked down in the ocean and they could hit Russian targets, and an Air Force that could fly them. So that in order for them to be safe, it wasn't good enough just to destroy the missiles in the silos here; but, yes, our reply, and this had to be—was that if ever the word came, that they had pushed the button, we had to set all of ours in motion.

Anderson: Do you think the Soviets understood this clearly?

Reagan: I have a hunch they did, yes, because I made it very plain to him—what we were gonna take and what we weren't going to take.

Anderson: You know, there's one other final thing I just want to mention here. A while back, I came to the White House when you were in the last few months with Ed Teller, and Lowell Wood of the Livermore Labs and Glenn Campbell came in, and they gave you a briefing on a new concept called brilliant pebbles. And first, just to bring you up to date, they're making enormous progress, and there's a good chance that they're going to make you look like a pessimist.

Reagan: Good lord, I bought their idea.

Anderson: No, but they are moving even faster than they thought they would.

Reagan: Oh, oh.

Anderson: They are [working] very rapidly to try and build one that will fly probably some time next year. And it's conceivable that if these little brilliant pebbles, these interceptors that can strike an enemy missile, [become a reality], you could in a short period of time make these big intercontinental nuclear missiles obsolete.

Reagan: That's what I'm dreaming of. That's the way to disarm, is to make them obsolete. But, yes, I didn't know—I'm not a scientist— how right they were, but I went to our people and . . . kept trying to sell this idea to them—because we were still in, you might say, in an experimental stage. We were researching as to was this right, and so the things that we had when we pictured them and things from space that would catch them there; then you would have a second echelon for those that got through up in space, and finally a third, just to try and catch them before they hit their target. I was pleased when I found out that the people who were doing the research and everything were fine.

Anderson: Can I tell you one quick, this is a story? I was on the General Advisory Committee for Arms Control, and I got a call and went to Livermore, and they had this incredible thing. And you know what their problem was? They couldn't figure a way to tell the secretary of defense or you what they were doing. And I talked to Glenn Campbell and he got hold of Ed Meese and they talked to Colin Powell, and they finally worked it in so you could find out what was going on. [Laughter]

There was a chance there they weren't going to tell you. But just to set the record straight: you then ordered them to move ahead and to examine that issue and explore it. It's beginning to have a dramatic impact.

Reagan: And then I actually paid a visit out in Colorado, to Martin Marietta, and I just was amazed at some of the things I saw, the progress that they had made. And I came away greatly encouraged that, yes, there is going to be a strategic defense.

Anderson: It takes a lot to make you look like a pessimist. [Laughter] One more question in the foreign policy area. When you look at the issue of terrorism, it seems to me that this is a special form of war and that American presidents are handicapped in this regard. There's one story about when, a few years ago, the terrorists in the Mid-East seized a Soviet diplomat and the Soviets very rapidly picked up a relative of the terrorist and executed him, and all the Soviets came right back and they haven't picked up another Soviet diplomat since. But we're constrained, you know: there are laws prohibiting any form of assassination by the CIA; you can't do that. Are we hamstringing our presidents, is there any case to be made that says in certain cases where the security of the United States is threatened or where you get some of these outlaw groups, that the CIA in certain extraordinary circumstances might need powers?

Reagan: All I can tell you is that actually we have been most effective. Now you haven't seen very many terrorist attacks here in the United States and in the world, I think we number in the hundreds those we have intercepted that never took place. We've had worldwide liaison with many of our friends in European nations and so forth, and we have been constantly intercepting messages and so forth getting on what's going on, and as a result have had a high rate of preventing. You can't prevent them all, just as you—

Anderson: And you don't get credit for that, either.

Reagan: No. Well, one of the reasons is that to get credit for it, you would have to expose what we were doing. Now, why did we know that we were going to punish Qadaffi? Because we had irrefutable proof, due to intercepted messages and so forth, that those two—the one in Italy where they came to the shoot out right in the inn and the eight-year-old girl was killed—well, we not only killed some but captured some of their men. And you know how simple it was there to fix the blame? Their passports for getting them into Italy were the same passports they had taken away from the Tunisian working men that they kicked out of their country, out of Libya, and they used them and gave them to these men. We have them. And the other one, the one in Germany, that one was through intercepted messages that we had. . . .

We picked out, as clearly as we could, targets that would minimize any killing of civilians in Libya. In fact, I think only one of the missiles missed its target and hit another target; then there was some death. But the rest of them were all aimed at Qadaffi's henchmen and Qadaffi's strongholds and so forth.

Anderson: So you basically think, as an American president, that our intelligence agencies work, that we're doing pretty well, that we can handle this and we're probably doing a pretty effective job.

Reagan: Yes.

Anderson: Now, let me, just turning to the whole world, some of the extraordinary things happening in the world today. A few weeks ago, I had a talk with Michael Halbouty. Remember him? The guy from Texas?

Reagan: Yes.

Anderson: He said, you know, Reagan broke communism. And one of the things I said in the book *Revolution* was that the ultimate irony of the 20th century may be that lasting worldwide political revolution was accomplished not by Trotsky and the communists but instead by Reagan and the capitalists. I've taken a lot of grief on account of that. But when you look around the world and you see capitalism spreading not only in Canada and England and France, but in New Zealand and Australia and the Soviet Union and China and even places like Angola and Hungary and Poland. What do you think about this? Do you think this is going to continue, and do you think that anything that you and your administration did in the last eight years had anything to do with it?

Reagan: Yes, I do. And part of it also was I think that Gorbachev was sincere about the things he's trying to get done, *perestroika* and all, because he inherited such an economic calamity. And that economic calamity was based on the amount of money they were spending on the military. So he means it when he says he wants to reduce weapons if he's going to, you know, change the system. But I do think that they've had 70 years of this one philosophy, and the hell of it is, it's brutal, it doesn't work. And here we are with two hundred years of a system, and I think it's just apparent that in the world today—it differs in some spots more than others—but there is this kind of awareness now that that system [communism] is not delivering.

But by the same token, there is awareness—when we came into office, less than a third of the people in Latin America lived in democracies. Today, 90 percent live in democracies or in countries moving that way, and I think it is just the plain proof, the evidence of one against the other. Now Gorbachev said to me in our first meeting, "I believe in communism." But, more and more, I think what he's saying is, yeah, but it's been mismanaged. He won't admit to being against the system. But look at his whole attitude. Could you figure several years ago, ever think of, a labor strike in the Soviet Union like we're seeing now?

Anderson: And that he gave in.

Reagan: Yes. There they are.

Anderson: Now, there are things going on that nobody could ever have predicted. When you talked to Gorbachev, or some of the Chinese leaders or Maggie Thatcher, did they ever indicate that the United States was the model?

Reagan: Oh, Maggie Thatcher has. Oh, yes. And others. I'll never forget at the economic summit seven heads of state were meeting, and I was the new kid in school. I can't remember which meeting it was, but it was when the '82 recession was over and all of a sudden our program was showing up. Well, I went to the summit meeting and sat there and there they were, the other six just sitting and looking at me. And then, one of them spoke up and said, "Tell us about the American miracle." You could look at Germany and others of those countries that had reduced their taxes as we did.

Anderson: Even Sweden.

Reagan: Yeah. They privatized. Margaret Thatcher is, well, she has done a better job privatizing than we have. She's turned those companies back into the private sector. And all of them are saying that. . . . And China, when we were there on the China thing and Deng Xiaoping and everything. There were the first signs, without their saying they were changing their system, but the first signs that they were moving this way. For example, they had a great pot of unemployed, but they had given an order out that any of those people who wanted to open a shop or a lunch counter or anything go ahead, and on the open market. You know, make money and keep it.

While we were there, I was told that there were no privately owned automobiles in China. They were all government vehicles. A family got together, pooled their resources and bought an automobile. And the government put them on television and said to the people, look, you too can work hard, save your money, and own an automobile.

Then we had a lunch that was arranged for us. And I could swear it wasn't a phony. They had already gone into the thing of now giving each farmer a portion of the land. These are on the collective farms. So that they had a farm of their own in addition to having to work on the collective farm.

Well, we had lunch in the new home of a farmer with him, his wife, and his little boy, that had been built from the proceeds of his private farm. He took us out on a little balcony on the second floor of the house and pointed out the dimensions of where his land ended and where the collective farm came in. Well, what's happened? There is no collective farm anymore in China. They found out that the others would produce so much that today they're producing four times as much as they were in agriculture. And doing it with these private farms. I'm sure this is what's got Gorbachev talking about lease holds for individuals, because he's seen what happened in China with the farms.

Anderson: Let me just wind this up. Two quick questions. Do you think this worldwide trend toward a greater degree of capitalism is a more lasting peace that is going to continue?

Reagan: Yes.

Anderson: And the final question, which I have to ask you. Relative to the books that have been written about you so far and the administration, what do you think of *Revolution*? Now I know yours is going to be better.

Reagan: [Laughter] What do I think of *Revolution*?

Anderson: My book.

Reagan: Oh, that's your book. Well I wrote you, didn't I, and told you, way back right after I'd finished it.

Anderson: I'm just wondering if you've had any second thoughts about it.

Reagan: Yours is the only honest book I've read about our administration.

Anderson: Thank you.

The Strategic Military Situation When President Reagan Took Office

by Lowell Wood

The world of strategic military affairs, as it confronted a new President Reagan in 1981 and as it evolved during his administration, was so very different than that with which most of us are familiar that basic aspects of it are already becoming nearly incredible. It may therefore be of value to review some of the salient—albeit arcane—features of this world before records of such thinly documented matters become even more obscure and memories of them fade excessively.

Origins of the Strategic Military Situation.   By the Reagan administration's outset, the Cuban Missile Crisis nearly two decades previously had lastingly impressed on the leadership of the Soviet Union the intolerability of being markedly inferior in military strategic nuclear capability to the United States. This time-stable leadership had been sponsoring a long-term program on historically unique scales to at least eliminate its inferiority—and presumably to attain superiority, if it were feasible to do so. This involved the establishment of programs to greatly accelerate the design, production, and operational deployment of a variety of strategic nuclear weapons and the means of delivering these weapons onto selected distant targets upon command.

Determinants of the Early Eighties Order of Planetary Battle.   By the early 1980s, the Soviet Union was producing strategic nuclear weaponry at several times the rate in explosive yield of the comparable US program. The Soviets had four independent ballistic-missile-production complexes in operation, each fielding a new generation of missile every several years. By contrast, the United States had a single, intermittently operating missile program, which was then producing launchers for the Trident seagoing ballistic-missile-deploying submarine fleet. When all components of strategic nuclear weaponry were aggregated, the Soviet Union had at least three times more "deliverable megatonnage"—the explosive yield of weapons capable of being dispatched to designated targets on the other side of the planet, given no interference by defensive countermeasures—than did the United States. This ratio was steadily increasing with time. As Harold Brown, the defense secretary in the Carter administration, had memorably testified before Congress, "When we build [long-range nuclear weapons-tipped ballistic missiles], they build. When we stop, they build."

Indeed, with the exception of the SS-25/Topol, the entire present-day Russian strategic order of battle, centered on the SS-19 and SS-18 "heavy" intercontinental ballistic missiles (ICBMs), each throwing, respectively, six to ten warheads of megaton-class yield, was represented as force-in-being to varying extents when Reagan entered the White House. The USSR's Typhoon ballistic missile-launching submarine force, still in service to a diminished degree in the Russian Federation's navy, became operational two years into the Reagan administration.

Moreover, the Soviets had also commenced deployment of an intermediate-range ballistic missile force, one centered on the road-mobile SS-20 missile and capable of striking any target in Western Europe from east of the Urals, at the beginning of the Carter administration and had completed most of this deployment early in the Reagan administration. While this three-warhead-throwing MIRVed missile (see below) was deemed to be an "intermediate range" one, it was revealed to also be a genuine ICBM capable of throwing one of its 150 kiloton (kT) warheads all the way to US targets, during the course of a famous "strategic surprise" Soviet exercise in April 1984.

The total lack of any missile defenses in either Europe or the United States, combined with the road mobility of the SS-20 launcher, made this particular nuclear weapons system—a system whose numbers peaked at over six hundred missiles and five hundred launchers—one that had *both* the precision-strike capabilities intrinsic in the high-quality type of land-launched ballistic missiles and the effective invulnerability to attack characteristic of the highest quality ballistic missile-launching submarines. It thus posed a remarkably sharp challenge to NATO forces, which were severely inferior in conventional arms to the Soviet-led Warsaw Pact forces facing them and which had hitherto depended on advantage in tactical nuclear weaponry as a "force equalizer."

During the Carter administration, NATO had offered to not deploy a countering intermediate-range nuclear missile capability, the Pershing II, if the Soviet deployment of SS-20s ceased. But this offer had been declined by the USSR before Reagan entered office.

MIRVing Implications. One of the most remarkable developments in ballistic missile technology in the 1960s and 1970s was the advent of the ability to deploy multiple warheads from a single rocket-launch vehicle, first in fixed patterns of multiple target-bombardment MRVs (multiple re-entry vehicles) and soon thereafter as sets of warheads, each one of which could be independently directed to any target within a reasonably wide-targeting area (MIRVs, or multiple independently targeted re-entry vehicles).

These technology advances—pioneered by the United States but quickly reproduced in the USSR—greatly increased the potency of ballistic missile attacks. The first generation of rocket-launch vehicles comprising the core of ballistic missiles had been built to carry very heavy warheads, so that their correspondingly high yields could compensate in terms of military effectiveness for the launchers' then-comparatively poor targeting accuracy. Thus the partitioning of the launch vehicle's payload mass budget, first into three, and eventually into as many as ten, distinct nuclear weapons atop a single rocket launcher of greater targeting accuracy sacrificed only modestly the realizable military effectiveness per weapon, while linearly increasing the number of targets that could be attacked using a single such launcher (whose cost dominated the cost of the total weapon system). This was due in significant measure to the fact that the multi-megaton-yield weapons carried by first-generation ICBMs were actually greatly oversized relative to optimum military efficiency in imposing damage on targets.

The highest-yield explosion that was still reasonably efficient in target destruction was of the order of a half-megaton in yield, with yields much above this level mostly going into "blowing the top off the local atmosphere," with little increase in military effectiveness. Thus a five-megaton yield bomb—comparable to that of the first Atlas ICBM, or its near-copy, the People's Republic of China's (PRC's) still-deployed CSS-4—could be partitioned into ten half-megaton bombs with almost a ten-fold gain in aggregate military effectiveness.

At least as important, such MIRVing gave any given rocket launcher a huge improvement in effectiveness in destroying enemy missile forces. If attainment of a genuine first strike capability were feasible, of two equal-sized missile forces, the one firing first could destroy its opposite number twice over, while still retaining 80 percent of its initial firepower. This basic numerical asymmetry contributed enormously to "strategic instability," in that it provided technically compelling incentives to striking first in any geopolitical crisis—as well as out of the blue. It also strongly incentivized the nation being attacked to "launch under attack," to use its strategic forces before they could be destroyed on the ground—although certitude of attack could never be perfect until bombs were bursting on their targets.

(To be sure, road-mobile rocket launchers were "differentially stabilizing" in that they seemingly couldn't be effectively brought under attack due to their in-principle forever-uncertain location and thus comprised a "secure retaliatory force." However, they weren't "absolutely stabilizing" if they were MIRVed—as most of them were and are—because each of them potentially could destroy multiple rocket launchers of the adversary nation.)

MIRVing of both US and USSR strategic missile forces had been essentially completed when Reagan came into office.

Strategic Forces Command and Control.   The strategic forces of both the United States and the USSR were commanded by a variety of means intended to ensure reliability of control under even the most demanding circumstances, when then-prevailing "military environments" might be severely uncongenial to essentially all types of communications. While US law and doctrine prescribed presidential control of strategic war systems, contingent arrangements necessarily had to be made lest physical destruction of the president or of his communications means disable the American systems via "decapitation" and, for instance, render any retaliatory attack infeasible. USSR arrangements were more permissive, with various levels of field commanders having "nuclear [weaponry] release authority" under various contingencies; in strategic-warfare jargon, these arrangements were deliberately made to be more likely to "fail deadly" under wartime circumstances, so as to make generation of conditions involving them less attractive to any adversary.

US strategic forces command-and-control arrangements during the Reagan era generally devolved down through the secretary of defense or his designated alternate civilian and onto senior general officers, eventuating with the commander of what was then the Strategic Air Command (SAC, currently the Strategic Command). If none of these survived—as might well occur in the case of a surprise attack from one or more offshore Soviet missile-launching submarines, or "boomers"—then command devolved to the senior officer on the NEACP, the National Emergency Airborne Command Post, which was expected to be sent airborne during even the less serious phases of a serious crisis, being aerial-refueled as necessary to stay aloft and presumably invulnerable to attack through the resolution of the crisis. In the later phases of any major attack, when the NEACP could no longer be fuel-supported and thus would soon become unavailable, the senior officer would presumably give final directions for continuing conduct of the war to surviving force commanders, relayed through surviving air and space platforms, many of which had been deployed by 1981.

Soviet arrangements for the conduct of strategic nuclear war apparently weren't quite as elaborate. The Soviet political leadership made extensive arrangements to depart central Moscow via dedicated, high-speed underground subways and trains, thence to be air-ferried by also-dedicated means to bespoke redoubts designed to survive even major attacks. From there some aspects of strategic forces command and control could be exercised, and the leadership could reasonably expect to emerge after cessation of large-scale combat.

As a back-up to these remarkably extensive leadership survival arrangements, the now-famous "Dead Hand" system, which purportedly would explicitly command most if not all Soviet strategic warfare systems to "fail deadly," was implemented (that is, weapons would be dispatched toward pre-selected targets automatically). To whatever extent the existence and operational doctrine of this system was made known in credible manners to US authorities, it presumably had a deterrent effect with respect to commencement of lethal attacks on the Soviet leadership, in an "*Après moi, le deluge*" sense. In any case, senior Soviet commanders apparently enjoyed extensive discretionary authorities—doctrinal, administrative, and physical—to employ strategic nuclear weapons systems under their command to considerably greater extents than did their American opposite numbers.

Soviet and American land-based strategic war systems—bombers and ICBMs—could be commanded redundantly and relatively readily with "ordinary" electronic means of extraordinary sophistication and "hardness." For example, the Internet grew out of the capabilities of the ARPANET initiative, an extensive US Department of Defense technology-demonstration project dating from the dozen years prior to the commencement of the Reagan administration. The project aimed at assuring functional integrity of worldwide communications with the SAC bomber fleet throughout the course of intensive, strategic nuclear war. (Of course, all fixed-site transmitters were vulnerable to attack, which was likely to take place in the earliest phases of combat. Thus they had to be highly redundantly implemented, as well as supplemented with mobile and space-based means of intrinsically greater survivability.)

The command of strategic forces housed in and carried on nuclear submarines at sea—the boomers mentioned earlier—was a quite different matter. As a militarily practical matter, boomers could be "spoken to" only via very low-frequency electromagnetic means capable of penetrating electrically conductive seawater to limited extents in order to reach slightly submerged towed antenna systems—the principal American approach. Or they could be spoken to via higher-frequency means requiring aerials penetrating into the air above the sea surface, the generally preferred Soviet means. (Both nuclear navies employed other approaches to various extents.)

The Soviet approach permitted much more extensive, higher-bandwidth communications, albeit at much greater risk of detection—and thus of compromise of the position of the highly vulnerable, relatively slow-moving submarine, bringing exposure to prompt or delayed destruction by anti-submarine forces in the area. As a consequence, Soviet use of aerials penetrating the sea's surface posed substantial issues of crisis stability to both sides, in that it was reasonably clear and probable that any first-strike-commanding message would be issued well in advance of Zero Time and that any retaliatory-strike orders would not be feasible due to destruction of land-based transmitter systems early in the war. Such apparent dedication of Soviet boomers to first-strike roles clearly incentivized American preemption against them in any strategic crisis—the more so as their positions generally were considerably better known to US anti-submarine forces than Soviet political and military leaderships had come to believe, at least through the long-running Walker-Whitworth betrayals. Of course, such pre-emption likely would swiftly induce large-scale strategic warfare, thus presenting a severe conundrum to all US military decision makers, starting with the president.

American senior commanders of the US boomer fleet were also confronted with the requirement to "speak" with extreme conciseness, due to the very limited bit rate of their mainline communications system, which required several minutes to globally broadcast a single, extremely compressed "Emergency Action Message" that contained coded wartime commands and authorizations to each and every American missile-launching submarine. The technical limitations of this system also precluded a response being sent back from

any of the US boomer fleet at sea, so that senior American commanders—including the president—were required to have extraordinarily
high degrees of confidence in the technical operability of their one-
way command communications links under wartime circumstances
never before experienced.

Attack Warning and Characterization Systems.   The USSR and
the United States devoted considerable efforts to gaining warning of
strategic nuclear attacks, both those about to commence and those
already underway.

Soviet efforts in this sector were largely limited to ground-based
radars that projected beams in the annular-spherical channel between
the Earth's surface and the Earth's ionosphere in such a manner that
they persistently covered US missile-launch areas, both land and sea
based. These radars would return characteristic signals if and when
missiles might be launched into and through this channel. When
Trident submarine capabilities gave the United States the ability to
launch from many areas in the world ocean, the Soviet response was
to deploy additional radar systems that looked in all directions from
which an attacking missile's warheads could possibly fly into the USSR.

The grave limitations of this approach were vividly demonstrated
in 1994, when a sounding rocket-launch being conducted for research
purposes by the Norwegians happened to occur in the line of viewing
of a major attack-warning Soviet radar watching the US Minuteman
ICBM field in Missouri. Although the Russian foreign ministry had
been given advance notice of this single-rocket launch per international agreements aimed at forestalling misunderstandings, this
information inadvertently wasn't conveyed to the defense ministry.
Commanders in the latter interpreted the unusual radar signals
received as indicative of a surprise Minuteman-carried attack being
launched from the United States, and prepared to launch a major
retaliatory strike, reportedly aborted with minimal time margins.

Recognizing these limitations of radar-only warnings of nuclear
attack, the United States had, well before the commencement of
the Reagan administration, come to employ "dual phenomenology"

means involving both long-range radar and sophisticated sensors of rocket-launcher exhaust plumes deployed in space satellites. These latter means proved to be highly effective, although the great expense of the satellites precluded much redundancy in their deployment and operations, so that transient outages frequently plagued the overall operational reliability of the system. That led to a few famous attack warnings being issued by the radar-only means when the space-borne means were returning either no signals or ambiguous ones.

These attack-underway warning means were nonetheless highly valued, as they could also serve to roughly characterize the attack, that is, to suggest whether it was light or heavy, and to prognosticate whether it was "counter-force" (directed against military forces and capabilities, including strategic attack ones) or "counter-value" (aimed at destruction of the most "value," that is, cities and populations) in nature.

The attack-underway warning means were always supplemented by "attack upcoming" warning means based on surveillance, especially electronic and space-borne sensors, of unusual activities on the part of adversary strategic forces and their operating personnel. Such means were expected to give several hours' advance notice of an attack being prepared, as the huge strategic war machines of the USSR and the United States could be thrown into combat operations by "pressing the red button" only in movies. (To be sure, ballistic missile-launching submarines were the notable exception to this "We'll always get tactical warning" presumption; they were—and are—intrinsically pre-generated and presumably could commence launching of their loads of ballistic missiles in a bolt-from-the-blue mode. Soviet boomers of the Reagan era were especially fearsome in this respect, as some of them had a demonstrated-in-action capability to "ripple-launch" their missiles in a sustained, closely spaced-in-time mode, so that a major attack involving nearly two hundred nuclear warheads could be launched by a solitary boomer stationed near US shores on single-minute time scales.)

An unfortunate feature of generating the strategic machinery to launch an attack was that it consumed a variety of essential commodities and expendables—including the availability of specialized personnel—that would require days to weeks to reconstitute if the attack were to be called off. This consumption became ever more notable as Zero Time approached, so that the "regrets" of an aborted strategic attack to the would-be attacker inescapably became ever greater. This of course contributed substantially to "deep-crisis" strategic instability: neither side could readily afford to run right up to the chasm's edge and then back away—or to believe such seeming backing-away actions on the part of the other side, as an interval of comparative strategic war incapability would inevitably ensue for the side backing away.

All incoming presidents—Reagan being no exception—are briefed on such commander-in-chief matters shortly before coming into office. Officers involved in such preparative briefings have informally indicated that their "pupils" have been quite startled and/or profoundly troubled by the information conveyed. (Perhaps such considerations partly explain why no senior US political official is known to have participated in strategic war exercises with senior military officers since Vice President Nelson Rockefeller did so in the mid-1970s. A notable American-Russian asymmetry is that all Soviet (now Russian) general secretaries and presidents routinely participate in nuclear war games and exercises with their senior military commanders; indeed, such jointly conducted political-military exercises are widely reported, complete with video footage, in the mass media of that country.)

Trans-Attack Decision Making and War Conduct in the United States. Once an attack underway was detected by surveillance means, it has been necessary—starting from well before the Reagan administration—to verify that it was real by reference to an entirely independent means, e.g., space-based assets if the primary attack-underway information had been sourced by long-range radars. Only after such dual phenomenology confirmation of a strategic attack being underway was in hand would the most senior US officers be convened via special-purpose teleconferencing arrangements in order to inform and advise the president and to receive his orders.

Damage Expectancies vs. Attack Types. An "Attack Conference" call, convened by senior commanders, had two items of business: the confirmation that a strategic nuclear attack was indeed underway and the assessment of its nature. By the time of the Reagan administration, it was believed by US strategic planners that reasonably likely Soviet attacks would at their outset be one of three types: counter-force, counter-value, and decapitation, in the jargon of the cognizant profession.

Counter-force attacks would be aimed at such serious attrition of US strategic nuclear capabilities that their use in retaliation against Soviet cities (Soviet military forces by then having been largely expended in combat or configured in wartime-hardness postures)—relative to the attack on American cities that would be essentially certain to occur—would be perceived to be futile; and thus no strategic nuclear response from the United States would be forthcoming. Counter-value attacks would be aimed at destruction of maximum value, i.e., would be city-busting ones aimed at eliminating the national population and the infrastructure that was capable of supporting large-scale military activities into the far future. Such attacks were prevalent in the latter days of World War II and were the "expected" type in the roughly 1945–65 time interval; but they faded in popularity with war planners as war goals became more sophisticated, e.g., the defeat (vs. utter destruction) of the adversary and the relatively unscathed survival of one's own country and people. Decapitation attacks were frankly aimed at so completely eliminating effective functioning of the National Command Authority—either by robustly destroying its topmost levels or by severing command connections between it and the strategic forces—that they became effectively incapable on time scales relevant to strategic conflict resolution.

It was estimated that the "incidental" loss of life in expected-to-succeed decapitation attacks might be in the low millions, that counter-force attacks (depending on their thoroughness) might impose total US casualties of ten to thirty million, and that counter-value attacks might involve 75–150 million Americans losing their lives, directly or indirectly, depending on the intensity of the attack.

Presidential Military Nuclear Decisions: Strategic.　In the final decades of the Cold War, presidential military nuclear decision making of a strategic—vs. tactical—character centered on the Stockpile Memorandum, the annual specification of the nuclear weaponry which the United States was to own in the coming years. The applicable law tasked the president with reviewing and approving the Single Integrated Operational Plan. The SIOP Book provided high-level specification for the conduct of various types and levels of nuclear war from the US perspective. (Soon after World War II, Congress basically signed over to the president the sole determination of the essentials of US nuclear strategy, confining its attention to the traditional Congressional concerns of specification, structure, governance, and funding of the armed forces, and the equipment, bases, and so forth thereof. Use of these forces in nuclear war was left largely—some might say nearly exclusively—to the president and defense secretary to determine, with Congress content to squarely assign these responsibilities to them by statute.)

Given his personal aversion to nuclear weaponry, President Reagan presumably found most, if not all, of the strategic nuclear decision making required of him to be disagreeable, especially those aspects of it that demanded personal public advocacy, that is, the deployments of the Pershing II intermediate-range ballistic missile (to threaten Soviet territory from NATO territory and thereby counter the previously deployed Soviet SS-20 missile force), the MX/Peacekeeper ICBM (to directly and reliably threaten—"hold at risk," in strategic warfare jargon—key Soviet military assets as well as the Soviet political leadership itself), and the commitment to produce and deploy the Trident D-5 sea-launched ballistic missile on extant US boomers (which resulted in the first-ever precision-strike capability from low-vulnerability sea-based platforms). Each of these three steps was bitterly denounced by Soviet leaders and their sympathizers abroad as driving superpower confrontation ever closer to the brink of war, as well as preparing for any of several strategic first-strike modalities.

Reagan's assurances that he was only creating bargaining chips to be traded away against corresponding reductions in Soviet strategic nuclear capabilities-in-being were very widely regarded as insincere—a viewpoint subsequently determined to be erroneous when the Pershing II deployment was reversed in exchange for the retirement of the SS-20 IRBM force and when the MX/Peacekeeper system was unilaterally retired over the past decade by the United States in response to budget-driven Russian ICBM forced reductions. In any case, the Pershing II and MX decisions were far more extensively decried by both foreign and domestic polities than any previous major strategic nuclear decisions had been, and thus it was unsurprising that Congress chose to participate in the details of the latter to quite unprecedented extents.

The annual Stockpile Memorandum review and approval was presumably comparably tedious for President Reagan, as it required him to approve each and every aspect of the US nuclear stockpile. That included the large number of new nuclear weapons of various types required to arm the several components of the Reagan defense build-up and the extensive testing of representatives of these weapons in underground nuclear explosions, as well as developmental nuclear tests aimed at ensuring against Soviet technological surprise in the nuclear weaponry sector.

However, the periodic presidential reviewing of the SIOP, for the conduct of all types of strategic nuclear war by all US military capabilities, was perhaps one of the most unpleasant aspects of the presidential command and control of the huge and complex American nuclear war-making system. The SIOP was—and is—in essence a menu for nuclear conflicts that contains the detailed specifications for all of the basic options cognizant military planning teams can think of that might be of interest to a president under all plausible geo-politico-military circumstances—including classes and intensities of conflicts around the world, weapons to be used against specific target sets, damage expectancies including casualty levels, and on and on. Disagreeable reading to all but the most hardened souls, it must have been exceptionally so to someone of Reagan's mindset regarding nuclear weapons.

All this considered, it's hardly remarkable that, when a senior aide inquired once in private as to what he would do if informed that a nuclear attack on the United States was underway, Reagan's response was in effect that he would have no choice but to retaliate in kind—presumably reflecting the realization that any other response would be instantly and enormously perilous to the United States and the prospects for maintaining an enduring albeit heavily armed peace.

Presidential Military Nuclear Decisions: Tactical.   When nuclear war would have been conducted via nuclear fission bombs carried in the bomb bays of long-range aircraft, for example in the early 1950s, a half-dozen hours of presidential decision time would be available during the early phase of nuclear war, and might be stretched indefinitely, if the president could flee successfully to a durable command post in the hours after long-range radars detected US-bound Soviet bombers. With the advent of Soviet ICBMs in the mid-1960s, the time scale shrank drastically, to the approximately 35 minutes required for an ICBM's warheads to fly from central USSR missile fields to US centers. This was still arguably sufficient time for a significant degree of presidential decision making, or even for a presidential flight to safety. The advent of Soviet boomers operating near the coasts of the continental United States (CONUS) in the 1970s compressed time scales another several-fold, depending on launch position and selected missile flight trajectory; e.g., depressed trajectory launches had smaller latencies attained at the cost of shorter available ranges. Fewer than a dozen minutes would elapse between the initial, necessarily provisional detection of a missile launch from a boomer in the vicinity of Bermuda and moderately high-yield thermonuclear detonations over Eastern coastal cities of CONUS.

The principal decisions to be made by a president when facing a nuclear attack center are how to react to it, e.g., with immediate or delayed response of what magnitudes, and with what nature of targets. Because presidential life expectancy under attack in the Reagan era might be denominated in minutes—the exception being the unlikely one of a credible attack warning becoming available sufficiently far in advance to enable his prompt flight to more durable circumstances— he would be expected to designate to his senior commanders one of a set of extensively prepared counterattack plans, lying before him as a consequence of previous SIOP briefings, and then to die very soon thereafter, as the "nuclear laydown on CONUS" commenced with detonations over the national capital region.

In actual practice, strategic war exercises in the timeframe of the Reagan administration rather uniformly indicated that, at strategic war's commencement, Washington, DC, would come under attack from warheads launched from Soviet boomers in the western Atlantic and that only eight to ten minutes would elapse from "missile break-water" until nuclear detonations commenced over the city. Several of these minutes would be expended in confirmation of the existence of the attack and assessment of its nature, in the course of convening the specified Attack Conference. They then would contact the president, advise him of the existence of the attack and its apparent nature, and ask for his directions.

Most, if not all, of these strategic war exercises—which included an officer deemed to have approximately the level of knowledge and decision making capacity of the president playing the role of the oft-awakened-from-sleep president—would still be informing him and responding to his basic queries regarding the attack when the first detonations occurred over the White House and the Pentagon, in spite of all involved being explicitly aware of the extreme time urgency of decision making. The final line of dialogue in such circumstances would be one of the most senior officers in the Attack Conference somberly saying something along the lines of, "Over to you, CINC-SAC. It's up to you now." The SAC's commander would then proceed to conduct the war as he thought best—conditioned by whatever guidance the president may have provided—for another six to eight minutes, until the nuclear detonations commenced over Omaha. National Command Authority, vested in the president a fraction of an hour earlier, then would devolve down onto the senior officer in NEACP, as noted previously.

Incentivizing "Good Nuclear Behavior" by the USSR Leadership. American strategic-warfare decision makers had exceedingly stark interests in forever persuading their Soviet counterparts not to launch nuclear attacks or to engage in behavior likely to lead to nuclear engagements. Through the commencement of the Reagan administration, efforts to influence such behavior had been along the lines of threatening to destroy assets believed to be prized by the Soviet government.

The Reagan administration elected to extend American deterrence to include the prospect of highly effective attacks on the most senior levels of Soviet leadership, via prompt precision strikes with high-yield warheads on their physical arrangements for survival under attack. The already significantly developed MX/Peacekeeper missile system was the chosen instrument, and its characteristics were unmistakably well-adapted for this purpose as well as others (including the "hard-target kill" of Soviet ICBM silos).

The Soviet leadership was understandably dismayed over this threat, never publicly stated, to their previously likely ability to survive a major nuclear war. This was in profound contrast to the long-held expectation of top levels of the US political leadership that most, if perhaps not all, of them and their families would likely die very early in any such conflict. The Soviets resisted the creation and deployment of the MX system by all (e.g., political and diplomatic) means available to them, albeit ultimately unsuccessfully; it attained operational capability in 1986.

The 500 high-precision, intermediate-yield (300 kT) MX warheads thus became one of the major stressors of Soviet politico-military power in the middle of the Reagan administration.

The Roles of (Novel) Active Defenses Against Strategic Missile Attacks. The first long-range ballistic missiles were the V-2s, pioneered and extensively used by the Nazis in World War II (producing more than six thousand and launching-to-targets more than three thousand), and subsequently deployed in lightly modified versions by both the United States (evolved into the Redstone) and the USSR (as the SS-1/Scunner, a precursor of the original SCUD-A) in the early and mid-1950s. While all three of these early deployments had chemical explosive warheads, the combination of long-range/low-latency strike and the enormous destructive capabilities of nuclear warheads swiftly made nuclear-tipped, long-range ballistic missiles the strategic weaponry systems-of-choice for most of the second half of the twentieth century. Such warheads were the essentially exclusive choice for longer-range ballistic missile armament as soon as they could be developed. They were highly evolved in both technological sophistication and quantities deployed by both the USSR and the United States at the commencement of the Reagan administration.

Large imbalances between defensive and offensive military capabilities never go unchallenged over long intervals, and the means of countering ballistic missiles were the subject of intensive study in the 1950s and 1960s. Major deployments of ABM systems commenced a dozen years before the start of the Reagan administration, following the inconclusive discussion of the missile-defense issue between US President Johnson and Soviet Premier Kosygin at the Glassboro Summit in 1967.

These systems were all direct conceptual and technological descendants of the anti-aircraft systems of World War II, centered on launching bullets against platforms, with proximity-fused "exploding bullets" being employed to compensate for far-less-forgiving inaccuracies in aiming during long-range, hypersonic-speed engagements. The most effective of these employed small (kiloton-scale) nuclear explosives against ballistic missile warheads soon to explode over or on their targets; the largest—intended to interdict clouds of a warhead plus decoys moving through space into defended target areas—employed multi-megaton explosives. The Soviets deployed many of the former type, deployments that quite handily survive into present times, while the United States deployed relatively few of both types and began shutting down these deployments soon after they had commenced, in the mid-1970s.

All of these early ABM systems had a one-on-one character, in that a single warhead of the offense was engaged by at least one counter-warhead of the defense—as the offense quickly spaced-out its echelons of attacking warheads so that no two of them could be neutralized by a single defensive counter-warhead. Indeed, the defense was typically compelled by considerations of technical and military operational imperfections to take at least two defensive shots at any offensive warhead, in order to gain a statistically acceptable likelihood of destroying it. The defense was further burdened by the often-severely disturbed battle environment within the Earth's atmosphere (the so-called terminal phase of defensive operations) which made it difficult to "see" the attacking warheads sufficiently well to be able to engage them effectively, while each of the ballistically aimed and/or inertially guided offensive warheads "knew" where they needed to go, from their long-ago-and-far-away launchings. Of course, the offensive ballistic-missile payloads could be made to attack in reasonably dense swarms—rather closely positioned in space and time. For the past several millennia, such "'offensive mass'" has been one of the most formidable challenges posed to any defense against any type of attack. Finally, the defense's engagement sensors for the out-of-the-atmosphere "midcourse" defensive battle-phase, with its intrinsically long ranges, tended to be high-tech and correspondingly delicate, while the offense's warheads could be configured to be enormously rugged relative to conditions in this arcane battle environment. As a result, the several distinct impacts of the "fog of war" typically would be far more severe for the defense than for the offense.

All such considerations taken into account, then, the classic missile-defense school of thought was hard pressed, as the Reagan administration commenced, to make a universally credible case for its likely military effectiveness against a still-burgeoning offensive ballistic-missile-technology-set.

President Reagan's senior officers of government—and occasionally Reagan himself—soon met up with members of the neo-classical school of ballistic missile defense, which contemplated a set of radical departures from previous approaches, ones specifically designed to either negate or actually invert the advantages hitherto enjoyed by the ballistic missile offense. These officers conveyed Reagan's privately issued call for a definitive, relatively near-term confrontation with Soviet power, and proceeded to authorize serious efforts directed toward effective elimination of the USSR's ballistic-missile threat.

Perhaps the single most drastic conceptual change contemplated in the offensive-defensive missile relationship was the commencement of the counter-attack against offensive missiles while they were still being launched—in the "boost" phase in which many warheads, typically six to ten, were clustered atop a single, slow-moving rocket-booster climbing into space out of a land-based silo or missile-launching submarine. Not only were these rocket boosters much more militarily fragile and far more readily seen from afar, due primarily to their very bright and unmistakable exhaust plumes, but they were also relatively few in number and high in both military and economic value: classic "fat, juicy targets." Such "carrying of the battle to the attacker" in a single stroke obviated the advantages conferred on the offense by MIRVing the rocket launcher's military payload: all the MIRVed warheads could be negated on the same launcher by a single defensive "shot."

A second radical innovation was the development of defensive weaponry that could engage many offensive launchers or warheads, either simultaneously or in such rapid sequence that many offensive targets could be engaged while any one of them was still vulnerable. This simultaneity or high concurrency of defensive capabilities proffered robust countering of offensive mass, and tended to invert the gross offense-defense asymmetry which MIRVing of offensive warheads had created. That this class of weaponry often operated at or near the speed of light itself potentially permitted the defense to engage the attack from defensive platforms located at great distances from the launch sites of the offensive rocket-boosters, so that they could be relatively secure—at least for the time being—against offensive countermeasures.

A third fundamental innovation was the introduction of comparatively very inexpensive, highly proliferated means of destroying ballistic weaponry in launch-phase, so that a unit of defensive effectiveness became at least ten times cheaper than the unit of offensive capability that it negated. This made it completely impractical for the ballistic missile offense to attempt to scale its way out of the dilemma newly posed by the neo-defense.

The Reagan administration embraced all of these approaches in its creation and emphasis on the Strategic Defense Initiative— " . . . to give us the means of rendering these nuclear weapons impotent and obsolete," as Reagan put it in his March 1983 speech—while stating the president's firmly held preference for missile-defensive means that involved no nuclear-energy release on any scale at any time. It presciently recognized that the corresponding R&D likely would be remarkably inexpensive—the SDI's costs never amounted to even 2 percent of US national security expenditures—and that even deployment of full-scale missile-defensive systems would cost at most a small fraction of what the more economically limited USSR had already expended to create the offensive capabilities, which would thereby be overcome and obviated. It was thus a deeply telling response to the long-term Soviet nuclear ballistic-missile enterprise, in which Soviet governments had invested substantial fractions of national GDP for preceding decades.

The Soviet response was to attempt to halt, slow, or constrain the realization of any of these systems by politico-diplomatic means, as the USSR leadership recognized from the outset that straightforward techno-military responses were not among available options. Reagan's personal determination to resist these Soviet attempts was pivotal—e.g., at the much-discussed Reykjavik Summit in 1986. His successful leadership of the US polity and the Western Alliance in marching forward along these lines so seriously impacted the Soviet worldview that first the Warsaw Pact and then the USSR itself crumbled under the combined psychological, economic and geo-politico-military stresses, of which the Reagan Strategic Defense Initiative was nearly universally acknowledged to be a pre-eminent feature.

The subsequent cancellation of the Strategic Defense Initiative by the incoming Clinton administration made the world once again safe for nuclear weaponry flung over intercontinental distances by rocket-launchers. Indeed, this situation continues through the present time, the remarkably expensive and ineffective missile defensive programs pursued by the Bush II administration notwithstanding. Thus it was quite unsurprising when the Russian Federation's leadership recently announced deployment commencement of two new classes of long-range ballistic missiles, one each land- and sea-based, and commencement of building a new class of ballistic missile-launching submarines—in spite of the greatly diminished total scale of the federation's military budget relative to those of Soviet times. As one of Reagan's senior advisors observed, "When you tax something, you get less of it; when you subsidize it, you get more of it."

Conclusion.   The Reagan administration played pivotal roles in the development of strategic nuclear warfare in many notable respects, the foremost of which of course was the bloodless culmination of the Cold War with the dissolution of the USSR-led Warsaw Pact. The administration also saw into existence the nuclear weaponry still central to the US strategic stockpile, i.e., the Trident D-5 warhead and the repurposed MX/Peacekeeper warheads now atop the correspondingly rearmed Minuteman ICBM force. An ironic consequence of US "victory" in the Cold War has been the freezing in place, qualitatively if not quantitatively, of most of the nuclear armaments of the Reagan military build-up.

Perhaps of comparable importance for the longer-range strategic nuclear-warfare picture, President Reagan personally tabled and eventually made credible—certainly to his Soviet opposite numbers, if perhaps only incompletely to his domestic critics—the still-startling concept of " . . . rendering these nuclear weapons impotent and obsolete," to quote his words again, via the Strategic Defense Initiative. This Reagan concept was shelved during the Clinton administration, after having been publicly accepted in 1992 by the Russian president as the basis for world-wide cooperative US-USSR defenses against ballistic missile attacks. The concept hasn't yet been effectively recommenced. It still may, however, prove to be a viable politico-military basis for moving into a future world in which strategic nuclear attacks—especially world-wrecking ones—are much less likely to occur.

Notes

ABBREVIATIONS USED IN THESE NOTES:

Bulletin = Bulletin of the Atomic Scientists

GPO = US Government Printing Office

Public Papers = *Public Papers of the President: Ronald Reagan, 1981–1989* (Washington, DC: Office of the Federal Register, National Archives and Records Service, General Services Administration). Also available at: www .reagan.utexas.edu/archives/speeches/publicpapers.htm [accessed June 18, 2014]. For other presidents cited: Public Papers of the Presidents of the United States [for the president cited]. Ed. by National Archives and Records Administration Office of the Federal Register (Washington, DC: US Government Printing Office).

RRPL = Ronald Reagan Presidential Library, Simi Valley, CA

Chapter One

1. Frank Newport, "Americans Say Reagan Is the Greatest US President," February 18, 2011. Accessed August 7, 2012. Available from www.gallup.com /poll/146183/Americans-Say-Reagan-Greatest-President.aspx.

2. Ibid.

3. Ibid.

4. Gallup Poll, February 6–7, 2009. Available at www.gallup.com/poll /114292/best-president-lincoln-par-reagan-kennedy.aspx

5. Question qn26e. 2012. Available by subscription at http://brain.gallup .com/home.aspx. In *Gallup Poll Social Series: World Affairs*: Gallup, Inc.

6. Jeffrey M. Jones, "Americans Judge Reagan, Clinton Best of Recent Presidents," February 17, 2012. Princeton, NJ: Gallup, Inc. Accessed August 7, 2012. Available www.gallup.com/poll/152771/Americans-Judge-Reagan-Clinton -Best-Recent-Presidents.aspx.

7. Question qn6a. 1993. Available by subscription at http://brain.gallup .com/home.aspx. In *January Wave 1*: Gallup, Inc.

8. Question qn3d. 2006. Available by subscription at http://brain.gallup .com/home.aspx. In *December Wave 1*: Gallup, Inc.

9. Question qn26e. 2012. Available by subscription at http://brain.gallup .com/home.aspx. In *Gallup Poll Social Series: World Affairs*: Gallup, Inc.

10. Jones, "History Usually Kinder to Ex-Presidents," April 25, 2013. Princeton, NJ: Gallup, Inc. Accessed June 25, 2014. www.gallup.com/poll/162044 /history-usually-kinder-presidents.aspx.

11. Quinnipiac University polls 1,000 randomly selected registered voters from across the nation. www.quinnipiac.edu/institutes-and-centers /polling-institute.

12. "Bush Tops List As US Voters Name Worst President, Quinnipiac University National Poll Finds; Reagan, Clinton Top List As Best In 61 Years." Quinnipiac University Polling Institute, June 1, 2006. Available at www .quinnipiac.edu/institutes-and-centers/polling-institute/search-releases /search-results/release-detail?What=best%20president&strArea=;&strTime =28&ReleaseID=919#Question005.

13. The December 2011 60 Minutes/*Vanity Fair* Poll. 2011. *Vanity Fair*, December 2011.

14. Ronald Reagan, *An American Life: The Autobiography* (New York: Simon & Schuster, 1990).

15. Lou Cannon, *President Reagan: The Role of a Lifetime* (New York: Simon & Schuster, 1991), 837.

16. Authors' conversation with Lee Edwards, Heritage Foundation, June 4, 2009. Edwards' biography was published in 1967 by Viewpoint Books, San Diego, CA.

17. *Reagan, In His Own Hand,* eds. Annelise Anderson, Martin Anderson, and Kiron K. Skinner (New York: The Free Press, 2001).

18. William Safire, "Reagan Writes," *New York Times Magazine*, December 31, 2000.

19. Godfrey Sperling, "Reagan Revisited," *Christian Science Monitor*, March 20, 2001.

20. *Reagan's Path to Victory: The Shaping of Ronald Reagan's Vision,* eds. Annelise Anderson, Martin Anderson, and Kiron K. Skinner (New York: The Free Press, 2004).

21. *Reagan: A Life in Letters,* eds. Annelise Anderson, Martin Anderson, and Kiron K. Skinner (New York: The Free Press, 2003).

22. Michael Duffy and Nancy Gibbs, "The Real Reagan," *Time*, September 29, 2003.

23. *The Reagan Diaries*, ed. Douglas Brinkley (New York: HarperCollins, 2007).

24. Reagan, *The Reagan Diaries*, Volume I: January 1981–October 1985; Volume II: November 1985–January 1989 (New York: HarperCollins, 2009).

25. *Public Papers of the President: Ronald Reagan, 1981–1989.* Available at www.reagan.utexas.edu/archives/speeches/publicpapers.html.

26. Martin Anderson and Annelise Anderson, *Reagan's Secret War: The Untold Story of His Fight to Save the World from Nuclear Disaster* (New York: Crown, 2009).

Chapter Three

1. Minutes of the National Security Council, December 3, 1981. In *Executive Secretariat, NSC: NSC Meeting Files: Records, 1981–1988.* RRPL.

2. Ibid.

3. Ibid.

4. Ronald Reagan, *The Reagan Diaries, Vol. I, January 1981–October 1985,* ed. Douglas Brinkley (New York: HarperCollins), 89.

5. "Statement on the Consequences of the Use of Nuclear Weapons." The Pontifical Academy of Sciences, Vatican City, Rome: 1981. Available at www .casinapioiv.va/content/dam/accademia/pdf/documenta3.pdf.

6. *The Reagan Diaries, Vol. I,* p. 93.

7. Minutes of president's working lunch with Agostino Cardinal Casaroli. December 15, 1981. In *Executive Secretariat, NSC: Subject File: Records, 1981–1985. Memorandums of Conversations—President Reagan* (December 1981) (1) (2). Box 49. RRPL.

8. *See* Paul Lettow, *Ronald Reagan and His Quest to Abolish Nuclear Weapons* (New York: Random House, 2005), 133.

9. Reagan Interview with Edmund Morris, The White House, Washington, DC, January 9, 1959. Accessed from the tapes of the interview in the RRPL.

10. The Nixon state dinner honored Mexican President Gustavo Diaz Ordaz. It was held in September 1970, at the Hotel del Coronado in Coronado, California. *See* Robert B. Semple, Jr., "Nixon is Host to the President of Mexico in California," *The New York Times,* September 4, 1970.

11. Reagan interview with Martin Anderson, Los Angeles, CA, July 25, 1989. Transcribed from tape. The full interview is printed in Appendix A.

12. Reagan was scheduled to give the lakeside talk at the Bohemian Grove on July 29, 1989. He had been a member of the club and its Owl's Nest camp since the 1970s, but did not attend summer encampments while he was president.

13. Reagan, *An American Life: The Autobiography* (New York: Simon & Schuster, 1990), 257–8.

Chapter Four

1. Ronald Reagan and Richard Gibson Hubler, *Where's the Rest of Me?* 1st ed. (New York: Duell, Sloan and Pearce, 1965).

2. Hans M. Kristensen and Robert S. Norris, "Global Nuclear Weapons Inventories, 1945–2013," *Bulletin of the Atomic Scientists* 2013 69:75. Accessible at http://bos.sagepub.com/content/69/5/75. The article is the source of the data in the chart.

3. Reagan, "Testimony Before the House Un-American Activities Committee." House Committee on Un-American Activities, *Hearings Regarding the Communist Infiltration of the Motion Picture Industry*, 80th Congress, 1st Session, October 23–24, 1947. Washington, DC: Government Printing Office, October 23, 1947.

4. Ibid.

5. Reagan, "McCarthy." Radio commentary taped May 8, 1979. Handwritten draft in "Personal Papers of the President." RRPL.

6. Dwight D. Eisenhower, "Address before the General Assembly of the United Nations on the Peaceful Uses of Atomic Energy," New York City. December 8, 1953. In *Dwight D. Eisenhower, Containing the Public Messages, Speeches, and Statements of the President, 1953–61*. Washington, DC: GPO, 1960, pp. 816–7.

7. Ibid, p. 822.

8. Evan Thomas, *Ike's Bluff: President Eisenhower's Secret Battle to Save the World* (New York: Little Brown, 2012), 184–6.

9. Eisenhower, "The President's News Conference, August 27, 1958." In *Dwight D. Eisenhower, Containing the Public Messages, Speeches, and Statements of the President, 1953–61*. Washington, DC: GPO, 1960, p. 640.

10. Kristensen and Norris, "Global Nuclear Weapons."

11. Eisenhower, "The President's News Conference," p. 649.

12. Kristensen and Norris, "Global Nuclear Weapons"

13. For example, his October 6, 1960, speech to the Women's Republican Club in Westport, CT, the text of which is available in the Reagan Library.

14. John F. Kennedy, "Statement by the President Concerning the Development and Testing of Nuclear Weapons, November 2, 1961." In *John F. Kennedy: Containing the Public Messages, Speeches, and Statements of the President*. Washington, DC: GPO, 1962, p. 693.

15. Kristensen and Norris, "Global Nuclear Weapons."

16. Lyndon B. Johnson, "Remarks Recorded for the Commissioning of the USS *Sam Rayburn*. December 2, 1964." In *Lyndon B. Johnson: Containing the Public Messages, Speeches, and Statements of the President*. Washington, DC: GPO, 1965, pp. 1,627–8.

17. Kristensen and Norris, "Global Nuclear Weapons."

18. Reagan, speech, "The Value of Understanding the Past." September 28,

1967. In Reagan Library Collection: *Governor's Papers, 1967–1975.* RRPL. Speech also accessible at http://www.ibiblio.org/sullivan/CNN/RWR /album/speechmats/eureka.html.

19. Kristensen and Norris, "Global Nuclear Weapons."

20. Richard M. Nixon, "First Annual Report to Congress on United States Foreign Policy for the 1970's. February 18, 1970." In *Richard Nixon: Containing the Public Messages, Speeches, and Statements of the President* (Washington, DC: Government Printing Office, 1971), 174.

21. Ibid, p. 173.

22. Kristensen and Norris, "Global Nuclear Weapons."

23. By the end of 1969, China had fifty nuclear weapons. They had built their first one in 1964. The United Kingdom joined the nuclear club in 1953, France in 1964.

24. Nixon, "Statement on Deployment of the Antiballistic Missile System. March 14, 1969." In *Richard Nixon: Containing*, p. 217.

25. Kristensen and Norris, "Global Nuclear Weapons."

26. US Department of Commerce, Bureau of the Census, "Vietnam Conflict—US Military Forces in Vietnam and Casualties Incurred: 1965 to 1972," table 428, *Statistical Abstract of the United States, 1973* (Washington, DC: US Department of Commerce, Social and Economic Statistics Administration, Bureau of the Census, 1973), 267.

27. Martin Anderson, *The Making of the All-Volunteer Armed Force* (Stanford, CA: Hoover Institution Press, 1991).

28. Ronald Reagan, "Letter to Holmes Alexander." Hoover Institution Archives, Hoover Institution, Stanford, CA, Ronald Reagan Subject Collection, Box 3, Folder RR Correspondence 1980. Quoted in *Reagan: A Life in Letters*. Ed. by Anderson, et al. (New York: Free Press, 2003), 533–4.

29. Lou Cannon, "The Reagan Years." *California Journal*, no. 5 (1974): 360.

30. Ronald Reagan, *Reagan, In His Own Hand: The Writings of Ronald Reagan That Reveal His Revolutionary Vision for America*, eds. Annelise Graebner Anderson, Martin Anderson, and Kiron K. Skinner. (New York: Free Press, 2001), 207.

31. Edward Teller, *Memoirs: A Twentieth-Century Journey in Science and Politics*. Ed. Judith L. Shoolery (Cambridge, MA : Perseus Pub., 2001), 509. *See also* Edward Teller, *Better a Shield Than a Sword: Perspectives on Defense Technology* (New York: The Free Press, 1987), 38.

32. Ronald Reagan telegram to William F. Buckley, November 6, 1973. In *Reagan, A Life in Letters,* 708.

33. Kristensen and Norris, "Global Nuclear Weapons."

34. *The New York Times*, "Transcript of Reagan's Remarks to the Convention," August 20, 1988, p. A-12. Accessible at http://www.reagan.utexas.edu /archives/reference/8.19.76.html.

35. Kristensen and Norris, "Global Nuclear Weapons."

36. Jimmy Carter, "North Atlantic Alliance Summit Text of Remarks on NATO Defense Policy. May 31, 1978." In *Jimmy Carter: Public Papers of the Presidents of the United States; 1977–1981* (Washington, DC: Office of the Federal Register, National Archives and Records Service, General Services Administration, 1977).

37. Kristensen and Norris, "Global Nuclear Weapons."

38. Reagan, "SALT Talks." June 27, 1978. In *Reagan, In His Own Hand*, pp. 79 and 82. Reagan's handwritten draft is pictured on pp. 80–1.

39. Martin Anderson, *Revolution* (New York: Harcourt Brace Jovanovich, 1988), 82–3.

40. Reagan, speech, "State of the Union," March 17, 1980. In Anderson, et al., *Reagan, In His Own Hand,* p. 475. The speech was delivered March 17, 1980, to the Chicago Council on Foreign Relations.

41. Cannon, "Arms Boost Seen as Strain on Soviets." *The Washington Post*, June 18, 1980.

42. Kristensen and Norris, "Global Nuclear Weapons."

43. Ibid.

Chapter Five

1. Hans M. Kristensen and Robert S. Norris, "Global Nuclear Weapons Inventories, 1945–2013." *Bulletin of the Atomic Scientists* 2013 69:75. Accessible at http://bos.sagepub.com/content/69/5/75.

2. Lowell Wood, "The Strategic Military Situation When President Reagan Took Office" (Appendix B in this book).

3. Reagan mentioned the 3-to-1 ratio in an April 1985 interview with reporters from *The Washington Post*.

4. "Toasts of the President and Prime Minister Margaret Thatcher of the United Kingdom at the Dinner Honoring the President, February 27, 1981." In *Public Papers*. RRPL. Accessed June 18, 2014. http://www.reagan.utexas.edu /archives/speeches/1981/22681e.htm.

5. "The President's News Conference, October 1, 1981. In *Public Papers*. http://www.reagan.utexas.edu/archives/speeches/1981/10081b.htm.

6. Ronald Reagan, *The Reagan Diaries: Vol.1: January 1981–October 1985*, ed. Douglas Brinkley (New York: HarperCollins, 2009), 52.

7. "Remarks and a Question-and-Answer Session at a Working Luncheon with Out-of-Town Editors, October 16, 1981." In *Public Papers*. RRPL.

Accessed June 18, 2014. http://www.reagan.utexas.edu/archives/speeches /1981/101681b.htm.

8. Reagan, *The Reagan Diaries*, p. 84.

9. "Remarks to Members of the National Press Club on Arms Reduction and Nuclear Weapons, November 18, 1981." In *Public Papers*. Accessed June 18, 2014. www.reagan.utexas.edu/archives/speeches/1981/111881a.htm.

10. "Minutes of Presidential Working Lunch with Augustino Cardinal Casaroli, December 15, 1981." In *Executive Secretariat, National Security Council: Subject File: Records, 1981–1985 Memorandums of Conversation— President Reagan (December 1981)* (1)(2). RRPL, p. 4.

11. "Minutes of the National Security Council, April 21, 1982." In *Executive Secretariat, NSC: NSC Meeting Files: Records, 1981–88*. RRPL, p. 6.

12. Ibid.

13. "Address before the Bundestag in Bonn, Federal Republic of Germany, June 9, 1982." In *Public Papers*. Accessed June 18, 2014. www.reagan.utexas .edu/archives/speeches/1982/60982b.htm.

14. "Question-and-Answer Session with High School Students on Domestic and Foreign Policy Issues, February 25, 1983." In *Public Papers*. Accessed June 18, 2014. www.reagan.utexas.edu/archives/speeches/1983/32583b.htm.

15. Ibid.

16. "Question-and-Answer Session with Reporters on Domestic and Foreign Policy Issues, March 29, 1983." In *Public Papers*. Accessed June 18, 2014. www.reagan.utexas.edu/archives/speeches/1983/32983a.htm.

17. Minutes of the National Security Council, November 30, 1983. "NSC00096 11/30/1983 [Strategic Defense] (1)(2)." In *Executive Secretariat, NSC: NSC Meeting Files: Records, 1981–88*. RRPL, pp. 4–6.

18. "Remarks and a Question-and-Answer Session with Reporters on Strategic Arms Reduction Talks, December 8, 1983." In *Public Papers*. Accessed June 18, 2014. www.reagan.utexas.edu/archives/speeches/1983/120883a .htm.

19. "Address to the Nation and Other Countries on United States-Soviet Relations, January 16, 1984." In *Public Papers*. Accessed June 18, 2014. www .reagan.utexas.edu/archives/speeches/1984/11684a.htm.

20. Reagan, "Interview with Robert L. Bartley and Albert R. Hunt of the Wall Street Journal on Foreign and Domestic Issues, February 2, 1984." In *Public Papers*. Accessed June 18, 2014. www.reagan.utexas.edu/archives /speeches/1984/20284j.htm. The transcript of the interview was released by the office of the press secretary on February 3.

21. "Remarks and a Question-and-Answer Session at Bowling Green State University in Bowling Green, Ohio, September 26, 1984." In *Public*

Papers. Accessed June 18, 2014. www.reagan.utexas.edu/archives/speeches /1984/92684b.htm.

22. "Debate between the President and Former Vice President Walter F. Mondale in Kansas City, Missouri, October 21, 1984." In *Public Papers.* Accessed June 18, 2014. www.reagan.utexas.edu/archives/speeches/1984/102184b .htm.

23. Ibid.

24. Minutes of the National Security Planning Group, December 5, 1984. In *Executive Secretariat, NSC: National Security Planning Group (NSPG): Records, 1981–1987.* RRPL, pp. 4, 5.

25. Ibid.

26. "Interview with Bernard Weinraub and Gerald Boyd of the New York Times, February, 11, 1985." In *Public Papers.* Accessed June 18, 2014. www .reagan.utexas.edu/archives/speeches/1985/21185d.htm.

27. "Interview with Lou Cannon, Dave Hoffman, and Len Downie of the Washington Post, April 1, 1985." In *Public Papers.* Accessed June 18, 2014. www .reagan.utexas.edu/archives/speeches/1985/40185d.htm.

28. "Remarks to Members of the American Legion Auxiliary's Girls Nation, July 18, 1986." In *Public Papers.* Accessed June 18, 2014. www.reagan .utexas.edu/archives/speeches/1986/71886c.htm.

29. "Remarks to Students from Southern Regional High School of Manahawkin, New Jersey, in Baltimore, Maryland, October 15, 1986." In *Public Papers.* Accessed June 18, 2014. www.reagan.utexas.edu/archives/speeches /1986/101586c.htm.

Chapter Six

1. Reagan wrote these talking points on a yellow pad. He kept the document after the meeting and took it with him when he left the White House in 1989. At Nancy Reagan's request, on October 4, 2000, Martin Anderson examined papers in Reagan's desk, which he was no longer using, and found this document. Accounts of the meeting from both the Soviet and American participants confirm that this is what Reagan said in the meeting.

2. Ronald Reagan, "Mr. Minister." In *Reagan, In His Own Hand: The Writings of Ronald Reagan That Reveal His Revolutionary Vision for America,* eds. Annelise Anderson, Martin Anderson, and Kiron K. Skinner, xxvi, 549. (New York: Free Press, 2001), 497.

3. "Informal Exchange with Reporters on Foreign and Domestic Issues, December 21, 1984." In *Public Papers.* Accessed June 18, 2014 at www.reagan .utexas.edu/archive/speeches/1984/122184b.html.

4. "United Kingdom: Prime Minister Thatcher Official Visit, 12/22/1984 (1)(2); Memcon: Ronald Reagan and Margaret Thatcher at Camp David." In *Executive Secretariat, NSC: VIP Visits: Records, 1981–1985*. RRPL.

5. "Remarks and a Question-and-Answer Session During a White House Briefing for Members of the Magazine Publishers Association, March 14, 1985." In *Public Papers*. Available at www.reagan.utexas.edu/archives /speeches/1985/31485a.htm.

6. Mikhail Gorbachev, "USSR General Secretary Gorbachev (8591009): Letter, General Secretary Mikhail Gorbachev to President Ronald Reagan, September 12, 1985." In *Executive Secretariat, NSC: Head Of State File: Records, 1981–1989*. RRPL.

7. "Minutes of the National Security Council, September 20, 1985. NSC 00121 09/20/1985 [Shevardnadze's Visit]." In *Executive Secretariat, NSC: NSC Meeting Files: Records, 1981–88*. RRPL, pp. 7–8.

8. *The Reagan Diaries: Vol. I: January 1981–October 1985*. ed. Douglas Brinkley (New York: HarperCollins, 2009), 508.

9. Reagan, "Handwritten Manifesto on Negotiating Strategy and Gorbachev, November 1985." In Reagan Library Collections: *Matlock, Jack F., Jr.: Files, 1983–1986*. RRPL.

10. "Geneva Summit Memorandum of Conversation. November 19, 1985: 3:40–4:45 P.M.: Second Private Meeting." In Reagan Library Collections: *Matlock, Jack F., Jr: Files, 1983–1986: Series III: US-USSR Summits, 1985–1986*. RRPL, pp. 6–8.

11. Martin Anderson's interview with Reagan, Los Angeles, CA, July 25, 1989. Published in full for the first time in this book. *See* Chapter 3 and Appendix A. Office of Ronald Reagan, Los Angeles; and Reagan, *An American Life: The Autobiography* (New York: Simon & Schuster, 1990), 637.

12. "Joint Soviet-United States Statement on the Summit Meeting in Geneva, November 21, 1985." In *Public Papers, 1981–1989*. Accessed June 18, 2014. www.reagan.utexas.edu/archives/speeches/1985/112185a.htm.

13. Gorbachev, "Text Excerpts from Gorbachev Arms Statement." Associated Press, January 16, 1986.

14. Gorbachev, "USSR: General Secretary Gorbachev: Letter, Mikhail Gorbachev to Ronald Reagan, June 1, 1986." In *Executive Secretariat, NSC: Head Of State File: Records, 1981–1989*, 7: Reagan Library.

15. *The Reykjavik File. Previously Secret Documents from US and Soviet Archives on the 1986 Reagan-Gorbachev Summit.* From the collections of The National Security Archive. Ed. by Dr. Svetlana Savranskaya and Thomas Blanton. George Washington University, Washington, DC: National Security Archive Electronic Briefing Book No. 203. Posted October 13, 2006. Accessed

August 12, 2012. *See especially* Document 6, "Gorbachev's Goals and Tactics at Reykjavik," National Security Council, (Stephan Sestanovich), October 4, 1986

16. Ibid, Document 6.

17. Ibid. *See especially* Document 5, "Anatoly Chernayev's Notes: Gorbahev's Instructions to the Reykjavik Preparation Group," October 4, 1986.

18. Ibid.

19. Ibid, "Transcript of Gorbachev-Reagan Reykjavik Talks," *FBIS-USR-93-087*, www.gwu.edu/~nsarchiv/NSAEBB/NSAEBB203/Document12.pdf, p. 6. Accessed August 12, 2012.

20. Reagan, "Address to the Nation on the Meetings with Soviet General Secretary Gorbachev in Iceland, October 13, 1986." In *Public Papers.* www.reagan.utexas.edu/archives/speeches/101386a.htm.

21. *The Reagan Diaries: Vol. II: November 1985–January 198*, ed. Douglas Brinkley. (New York: HarperCollins, 2009), 792.

22. The treaty was ratified by the US Senate on May 27, 1988, and came into force only a few days later. Under the treaty, by June 1, 1991, a total of 2,692 nuclear weapons had been destroyed—846 by the United States and 1,846 by the Soviet Union. *See* Federation of American Scientists, http://fas.org/nuke/control/ /intro.htm.

Chapter Seven

1. "Minutes of the National Security Planning Group, February 9, 1988." NSC System II 90141. RRPL, p. 2.

2. Ibid, p. 3.

3. Ibid, p. 4.

4. Ibid, p. 8.

5. "Minutes of the National Security Planning Group, May 23, 1988: US Options for Arms Control at the Summit." In *Executive Secretariat, NSC: System Files: Records, 1981–89.* RRPL, 1988, p. 2.

6. "Joint Statement Following the Soviet-United States Summit Meeting in Moscow, June 1, 1988." In *Public Papers.* Accessed June 18, 2014. http://www.reagan.utexas.edu/archives/speeches/1988/060188b.htm.

7. Ibid.

8. "Address to the 43d Session of the United Nations General Assembly in New York City, September 26, 1988." In *Public Papers.* Accessed June 14, 2014. www.reagan.utexas.edu/archives/speeches/1988/092688.htm.

9. "Statement on the Soviet-United States Arms Control Negotiations, November 16, 1988." In *Public Papers.* Accessed June 14, 2014. www.reagan.utexas.edu/archives/speeches/1988/111688c.htm.

10. "The President's Private Meeting with Gorbachev," December 7, 1988,

1:05–1:30 p.m., commandant's residence, Governor's Island, New York." In *Reagan, Gorbachev and Bush at Governor's Island: Previously Secret Documents from Soviet and US Files On the 1988 Summit in New York, 20 Years Later*, Document 8: Memorandum of Conversation. From the collections of The National Security Archive. George Washington University: Washington, DC., Electronic Briefing Book No. 261, ed. by Dr. Svetlana Savranskaya and Thomas Blanton. Posted December 8, 2008. Obtained via the Freedom of Information Act from the RRPL.

Chapter Eight

1. Ronald Reagan, "Handwritten Manifesto on Negotiating Strategy and Gorbachev, November 1985." In *Collection of Jack F. Matlock Jr.*, Ronald Reagan Presidential Library. Simi Valley, CA.

2. Francis X. Clines, "A Neocapitalist Basks with Reagan," *The New York Times*, May 5, 1992, p. A3.

3. Reagan, "Remarks at Presentation of Ronald Reagan Freedom Award to Mikhail Sergeyevich Gorbachev, May 4, 1992." Ronald Reagan Presidential Library, Simi Valley, CA.

4. Ibid.

5. Ibid.

Chapter Nine

1. *President Mikhail Gorbachev: Keynote Speech at Ronald Reagan Day Dinner of Eureka College*. Eureka, IL: Eureka College Archives, 2009, p. 7.

2. Ronald Reagan, "Address Before the Japanese Diet in Tokyo, November 11, 1983." In *Public Papers*. Accessed June 18, 2014. www.reagan.utexas.edu/archives/speeches/1983/111183a.htm..

3. Reagan, "Address Before a Joint Session of the Congress on the State of the Union, January 25, 1984." In *Public Papers*. Accessed June 18, 2014. www.reagan.utexas.edu/archives/speeches/1984/12584e.htm.

4. *President Mikhail Gorbachev's Remarks at the Eureka College Convocation Ceremony*. Eureka, IL: Eureka College Archives, 2009, p. 8.

5. Stephen F. Cohen and Katrina vanden Heuvel, "Gorbachev on 1989," *The Nation*, November 16, 2009, pp. 11–16.

Chapter Ten

1. George H. W. Bush, "The President's News Conference, January 27, 1989." In *Public Papers: George Bush: 1989 (Book 1)*, 1990.

2. Hans M. Kristensen and Robert S. Norris, "Global Nuclear Weapons Inventories, 1945–2013," *Bulletin* 2013 69:75. Accessed June 18, 2014. http://

bos.sagepub.com/content/69/5/75. *See also* Robert S. Norris and Hans M. Kristensen, "US Nuclear Forces, 2010." 66, no. 3, pp. 57–71; and Norris and. Kristensen, "Russian Nuclear Forces, 2010," *Bulletin of the Atomic Scientists* 66, no. 1, pp. 74–81.

3. George H. W. Bush, "Remarks at the Annual Conference of the Veterans of Foreign Wars, March 6, 1989." In *Public Papers 1989 (Book 1)*, 1990, p. 176.

4. George H. W. Bush, "Remarks at the United States Coast Guard Academy Commencement Ceremony in New London, Connecticut, May 24, 1989." In *Public Papers 1989*, 1990, p. 603.

5. George H. W. Bush, "The President's News Conference Following the North Atlantic Treaty Organization Summit Meeting in Brussels, May 30, 1989." In *Public Papers 1989 (Book 1)*, 1990, p. 638.

6. Dan Goodgame and Michael Duffy, "Read My Hips," *Time*, October 22, 1990, p. 26.

7. William J. Clinton, "Remarks to the Community, in Los Alamos, New Mexico, May 17, 1993." In *Public Papers 1993 (Book 1)*, 1994, pp. 974–7.

8. Clinton, "Statement on Comprehensive Nuclear Weapons Test Ban Negotiations, August 11, 1995." In *Public Papers 1995 (Book 2)*, 1996, p. 1,251.

9. George W. Bush, "Remarks at the National Defense University, May 1, 2001." In *Public Papers 2001*, p. 473.

10. Bush spoke at the National Defense University on October 23, 2007. The text is available at http://2001-2009.state.gov/r/pa/ei/wh/94059.htm.

11. Shannon N. Kile and Hans M. Kristensen, "World Nuclear Forces, 2005." In *SIPRI Yearbook 2005*, Appendix 12A, p. 580. Stockholm International Peace Research Institute. Accessed June 28, 2014. http://www.sipri .org/yearbook/2005/files/SIPRIYB0512A.pdf.

12. George W. Bush, "Remarks at the US Military Academy at West Point in West Point, New York, December 9, 2008." In *Public Papers 2008 (Book 2)*, 2009, pp. 1,503–8.

13. Barack Obama, "Remarks in Prague, April 5, 2009." In *Public Papers 2009 (Book 1)*, pp. 439–44.

14. Kristensen and Norris, "Global Nuclear Weapons Inventories."

Chapter Eleven

1. Federation of American Scientists, "Status of World Nuclear Forces 2014." Available at www.fas.org/programs/ssp/nukes/nuclearweapons/nuke status.html. Updated April 30, 2014. Accessed June 18, 2014.

2. Hans M. Kristensen and Robert S. Norris, "Global Nuclear Weapons Inventories, 1945–2013," *Bulletin of the Atomic Scientists* 2013 69:75. Accessed June 18, 2014. http://bos.sagepub.com/content/69/5/75.

3. Ibid, p. 75.

4. Ibid, p. 77.

5. Sidney P. Drell is professor of theoretical physics (emeritus) at the Stanford Linear Accelerator Center and a senior fellow at the Hoover Institution. George P. Shultz, who served as Reagan's secretary of state, is the Thomas W. and Susan B. Ford Distinguished Fellow at the Hoover Institution.

6. *Implications of the Reykjavik Summit on Its Twentieth Anniversary: Conference Report,* eds. Sidney D. Drell and George P. Shultz (Stanford, CA: Hoover Institution Press, 2007), 101. The conference was held October 10–12, 2006, at the Hoover Institution. Participating were Martin Anderson, Steve Andreason, Michael Armacost, Admiral William Crowe, Sidney Drell, James Goodby, Thomas Graham, Thomas Henriksen, David Holloway, Max Kampelman, Jack Matlock, John McLaughlin, Don Oberdorfer, Richard Perle, William Perry, Peter Robinson, Harry Rowen, Scott Sagan, Roald Sagdeev, George Shultz, Abe Sofaer, and James Timbie.

7. Philip Taubman provides a complete account in *The Partnership: Five Cold Warriors and Their Quest to Ban the Bomb* (New York: Harper, 2012), 309.

8. George Shultz, Henry Kissinger, Sam Nunn, and William Perry, "A World Free of Nuclear Weapons, *The Wall Street Journal,* January 4, 2007, p. A15.

9. Mikhail Gorbachev, *The Wall Street Journal,* January 31, 2007, p. A13.

10. Martin Anderson's interview with Ronald Reagan, Los Angeles, July 25, 1989, quoted in Chapter 3.

About the Authors

Martin Anderson (1936–2015), who served as the Keith and Jan Hurlbut Senior Fellow at the Hoover Institution, Stanford University, and **Annelise Anderson**, a research fellow at Hoover, are recognized experts on the writing and speeches of Ronald Reagan. They are the authors of several bestselling books that quote from and analyze the late president's thousands of handwritten radio commentaries, letters, speeches, and notes that document his personal and professional journey in his own words. The Andersons' most recent book is *Reagan's Secret War: The Untold Story of His Fight to Save the World from Nuclear Disaster.*

Both Martin and Annelise Anderson worked for Reagan in his 1976 campaign for the Republican presidential nomination and in his 1980 campaign four years later. They also served on the 1980 presidential transition team and in the Reagan White House. Martin Anderson was assistant to the president for policy development, where he worked with the president on policy issues on a daily basis.

Annelise Anderson was associate director of the Office of Management and Budget, where she was responsible for the budgets of five cabinet departments and 40 other agencies.

Lowell Wood, who wrote Appendix B, is an expert on strategic systems having national security significance. Formerly on the staff of the Lawrence Livermore National Laboratory, he has, over the years, advised many policy makers on weapons and strategy.

Index